HARLEY-DAVIDSON

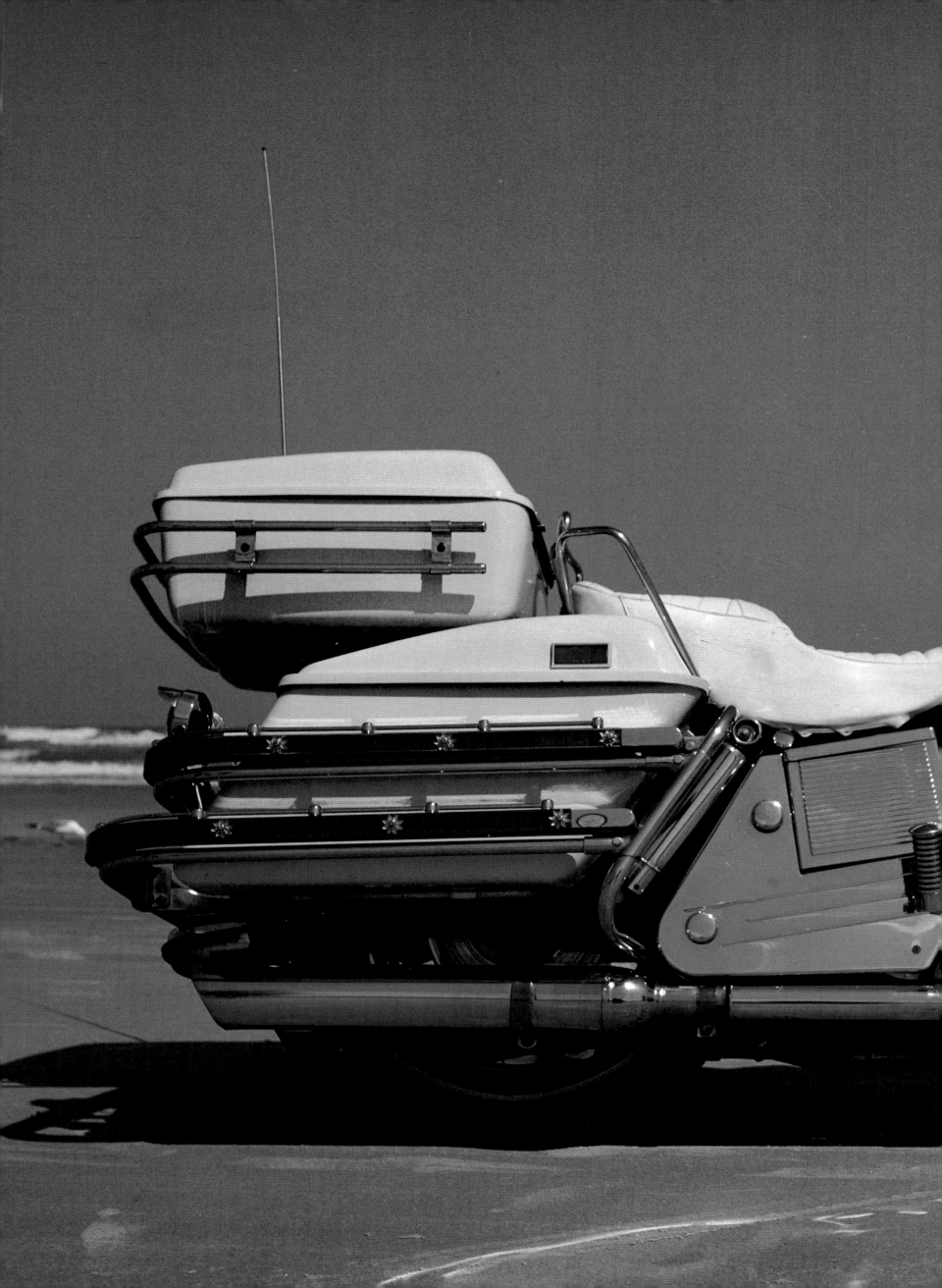

HARLEY-DAVIDSON

TONY MIDDLEHURST

SMITHMARK

This edition published in 1994
by SMITHMARK Publishers Inc.,
16 East 32nd Street
New York, New York 10016.

SMITHMARK books are available for bulk purchase for sales promotion and premium use. For details write or telephone the Manager of Special Sales, SMITHMARK Publishers Inc., 16 East 32nd Street, New York, NY 10016. (212) 532-6600.

Produced by Brompton Books Corp.,
15 Sherwood Place,
Greenwich, CT 06830.

ISBN 0-8317-4293-3

Printed in Spain

10 9 7 6 5 4 3 2

Page 1: Power and beauty...Rivera-carbed Evolution Low Rider ticks at rest after a leisurely cruise in the sun.

Pages 2-3: Archetypal Harley: the gold, chrome and white leather excess of a '76 Electra Glide in a classic setting – Daytona Beach.

Below: Everyone's dad knows at least one story about a guy who took despatches to the front line on one of these – the ever-dependable WLA45 (1942).

Contents

Introduction

I'll never forget my first ride on a Harley.

It was the back end of the 1970's, when the summers seemed so much hotter and the roads so much more open. I was a callow youth then, still buzzing with the adrenalin – and the disbelief – that came from having landed a job as assistant road tester on a motorcycle magazine. I'd been 'broken in' on a succession of mind-numbingly quick Japanese superbikes, until finally I was ready to be trusted with my first 'hog' – a cherry red 1000cc Sportster.

Nothing that I had sampled before could have prepared me for the other-worldliness of that Sportster. Crimson peanut tank set off by acres of chrome, crude V-twin motor leaping about (rather alarmingly, it seemed) inside an impossibly spindly frame, freeway forks plunging and heaving in protest at the English A-roads, rock-hard seat and suspension pummelling my spine . . . Right then, the Sportster seemed about as inaccurately named as any motorcycle could be. Agricultural, noisy, thirsty, uncomfortable – it was the ultimate in excess. And I loved it.

I loved it even when, less than two miles into what was supposed to be an uplifting ride down to the Sussex coast (shared by an at first reluctant lady passenger), the clip holding the exhaust pipes together fell off. One piece of bent wire and several burned fingers later, the bike sounded disturbingly like an ailing World War II bomber, but at least we were rolling again. The lady was less than impressed, so I cut my losses and headed home. Just as well, since the clutch lever was so unbelievably heavy that I had been in some serious doubt about the long-term health of my left wrist.

Before the Evolution motor came along in the early 1980s, it had never been an easy job defending Harleys against their many detractors. Things are different now, of course. Now H-Ds can stand comparison with a surprisingly wide cross-section of competitors. But in nearly ninety years of continuous manufacture, the world's most famous and charismatic motorcycle company has always had a devout following among motorcyclists who recognise (and can afford to pay for) that certain indefinable quality which sets the Milwaukee machines apart from the rest.

In my time on *SuperBike* magazine, I lost count of the number of times photographic sessions involving test Harley-Davidsons were interrupted by members of the public. Misty-eyed men seemed to appear from out of nowhere, each of them with an H-D anecdote to retell. No other test bikes ever aroused anywhere near the same level of awed curiosity as Harleys did.

I always listened to those fellows, on the basis that I'll end up the same way when I'm an old man . . . and then I'll need someone to listen to *my* anecdotes.

Did I ever tell you about the time I was riding an '84 Low Rider across the Arizona desert, for example? Now, *that* was an adventure . . .

Whether you're a racer or an antique collector, a loner or a club rider, there is a motorcycle with the words 'Harley-Davidson' written on the tank just waiting for you. Pictured here are the storming XR750 dirt trackers, the classic '30s knucklehead and the buddy seat and tank emblem which set all Harleys apart in a crowd.

Three Men and a Shed

History abounds with stirring 'rags to riches' tales of successes achieved through adversity, of triumphs snatched from the jaws of disaster, of fulfilments forged on the unlikeliest of anvils.

The Harley-Davidson story is a classic example of this genre. Despite two world wars and several economic depressions, both global and local, the world's most charismatic motorcycle manufacturer has survived intact, right through to the present day. In truth, to regard it as merely survival is to understate the magnitude of H-D's achievement over some ninety years of existence. The extraordinarily humble nature of the company's beginnings in the first decade of the twentieth century only serves to add extra poignancy to the robustly healthy situation in which Harley-Davidson now finds itself.

Despite the best efforts of ever more aggressive opposition, Harley-Davidson have flourished. Ironically, the springboard for the present prosperity – which could not have been predicted by the most optimistic of observers as recently as the 1960s – did not result from slavish pursuit of the 'if you can't beat 'em, join 'em' philosophy resignedly adopted in the 70s and 80s by other, non-Japanese motorcycle manufacturers. Rather, it has been secured through a dogged determination – at times perceived by industry pundits as bordering on the suicidal – to stick with the original values of strength and simplicity embraced by the factory founders all those years ago. Now, Harley-Davidson are well placed to move confidently towards the next century, building on their curiously traditional (some would say old-fashioned) range of motorcycles – and on one of the most potent product images in history.

This image, a particular quality exclusive to Harley-Davidson which is as hard to define as it is easy to recognise, has in the past formed the basis of countless treatises and dissertations by writers, academics, psychologists and even theologians. It is a quality spread over a wide canvas, defying categorisation and transcending all barriers. Old or young, enthusiast or antago-

nist, advertising copywriter or abbatoir cleaner – not matter what your social class or upbringing might be, the name of Harley-Davidson is almost certain to evoke some kind of response.

Like Band-Aids, Harleys have gradually assumed a near-generic identity in the public's mass consciousness. Even the frailest of grandmothers knows that a Harley-Davidson is a motorcycle; how many would know the same of a Kawasaki? At the other extreme, there are groups of diehards who refuse to acknowledge the existence of any other make of motorcycle, such is their blind allegiance to the Harley creed. And creed is not too strong a word in the opinion of those whose entire lifestyle is based on the near-religious experience of riding in a pack of thundering H-Ds. When it bites, the Harley bug bites deep.

It is unlikely that William S Harley or his ex-schoolchum Arthur Davidson anticipated such a degree of reverence being accorded to their products when, in 1903, they stood back to admire the first fully-mobile fruits of their labors. As so often seems to be the case with individuals and companies that later go on to achieve great fame, there were no shining beacons, flashes of light or thunderclaps of inspiration at the beginning of Harley-Davidson's history, no indications as to what might happen in the future. Few could have foreseen a time when decisions concerning the future of Harley-Davidson would be taken by no less a personage than the President of the United States, so great would be the importance attached to what had by the 1980s become one of the most sacrosanct of America's national institutions.

Interestingly enough, although Harley-Davidsons have always been ranked right up alongside apple pie and bald eagles in terms of their 'American-ness' – even the corporate logo is an unashamed clarion call to patriotism – the American lineage of both Harley and Davidson could hardly have been shorter. William Harley was born in Milwaukee in 1880, son to one of the many couples who had emigrated from England (in Harley's case, from

Left: Walter Davidson Snr with one of the early singles which helped build H-D's reputation as a manufacturer of sturdy (if somewhat unadventurous) machines in the early part of this century.

Right: Bill Harley's engineering skills were honed in a Milwaukee pedal cycle factory before he made the big jump to motorisation. This early publicity shot, taken outside Hirsch's Harley dealership in Seattle, acknowledged and paid homage to this heritage.

Previous page: If the lack of brakes didn't kill them, the punctures caused by wood splinters probably would. . . . American board-racing velodromes in the 1910s and '20s were battlegrounds for only the bravest Harley men.

the industrial north-west) at around that time. Arthur Davidson's American antecedence was just as shallow, his parents having shipped out from Aberdeen, Scotland only ten years before his birth in 1881. His was a family of three boys and two girls; all three brothers would go on to become founder members of the Harley-Davidson Motor Company.

But that was later. In the beginning, it was Arthur Davidson and Bill Harley who fired up the operation. With hindsight, bearing in mind their shared interests in bicycles and in the still new four-stroke internal combustion engine, it was perhaps inevitable that they would form a partnership to produce motorcycles. And yet, in another of these strange and unexpected twists which shape the genesis of great companies and institutions, it appears from the scanty records extant from this period that boats came before bikes in the history of Harley-Davidson.

The crucial turn of fate which effectively ushered in the H-D dynasty was Bill Harley's decision to sharpen up his fitter's skills (which up to then had been put to good use in one of Milwaukee's bicycle works) by taking up a draftsman's apprenticeship at the nearby Barth Manufacturing Company. Already holding down a patternmaker's job at the same metalworking shop was Arthur Davidson.

Their schoolboy friendship was quickly rekindled, as was their mutual interest in the outdoor life. Lying on the western banks of lake Michigan, hard by many other smaller lakes, Milwaukee was a handy base of keen anglers like Bill and Art. The two teenagers made numerous fishing trips together in a small rowboat, regretting only the fact that their sphere of activity was necessarily limited by their boat's restricted range. The prime fishing areas, in the outlying tributaries and deep water zones, were always out of reach.

At this time, in the final years of the nineteenth century, the dominant and most copied automotive engine was the seminal four-stroke single created in 1895 by Frenchmen Count Albert de Dion and Georges Bouton. Also at this time, as luck would have it, another (rather less well-known) European was working at Barths. There was nothing particularly extraordinary or remarkable about Emil Kruger. He was German, but then so were many of the men who had left Europe in the late nineteenth century to look for fame and fortune in America's 'boiler room', the north-central industrial heartland of Wisconsin, Illinois and Michigan.

What made Kruger interesting to the two young men from Milwaukee was the fact that he had brought with him some detailed construction plans for a De Dion-type engine from Aster, his previous employers in Paris. With Kruger's cooperation, Harley and Davidson set to work building a short series of motors, culminating in one which turned out to be a more than adequate power source for their fishing boat.

Although this was their first and last direct involvement in the marine world, the watery connection did not disappear entirely. While working on separate freelance engineering assignments prior to the formation of the Harley-Davidson Motor Co., Arthur Davidson collaborated extensively with another young engine 'nut' by the name of Ole Evinrude. The Evinrude badge would later become synonymous with powerful outboard motors for sports and leisure marine craft.

Back in 1900, having cracked the fishing problem, Harley and Davidson were turning their attentions back towards dry land, and specifically towards the commercial potential of a motorised bicycle. Reasoning, with some justification, that they were unlikely to reach a standard any lower than that already being displayed by a disturbingly large number of 'get-rich-quick' manufacturers, whose expertise seemed to lie more in the fields of charlatanry and intrigue than in engineering, Bill and Arthur began to develop their own engines, based once more on Kruger's Aster/De Dion plans.

Arthur's parents proved supportive of their son's ambitions. This was fortunate, since all the development work was going on inside their respectable middle-class Milwaukee home. Art's elder brother Walter, up to then working as a railroad machinist in the great empty wastes of the central United States, got wind of all the feverish activity and decided in 1902 to return to the homestead for a piece of the action, albeit in a part-time role. This 50 percent boost to the staff complement was both helpful and at the same time awkward, since it put near-intolerable extra strain on the already cramped working conditions.

Harley was able to come up with some temporary relief in the shape of a friend's workshop. That was enough to bring about the existence, in the spring of 1903, of the first fully-functioning cycle powered by a Harley-Davidson motor – or at any rate, by a motor bearing the name of Harley-

Above: A typical 5-35 type single, as produced in considerable numbers (and with little modification) between 1904 and 1918. Relatively good silencing and a conservative paint scheme earned it the nickname 'Silent Gray Fellow'.

Right: Indian's high-tech racers were a thorn in Harley's flesh for decades. This confident pilot is about to try his luck at Brooklands in 1911.

Davidson on its crankcase. The engine broke no new ground; it was a conventional single, featuring the so-called 'atmospheric' valve arrangement typical of the day (the valves' function being controlled purely by the movement of gases inside the combustion chamber). It displaced around 400cc. This power unit was fitted into its guinea-pig cycle frame by the simple expedient of bolting it into the space beneath the crossbar, a logical design whose precedent had been successfully set one year before by George Hendee and Oskar Hedstrom in Springfield, Massachusetts in the construction of the first 'Indian' motorcycle.

Although the concept was admirable in its simplicity, it soon became clear to the H-D men that an arrangement where the power source was considerably more potent than that of the average human being's leg muscles invariably brought destructive forces to bear on the bicycle's now-overstressed parts. Breakages were frustratingly frequent in the early stages of testing, and the situation was in no way improved by the imperfect condition of American roads at the time.

Assuming they were of serious intent, and wishing to sell machines in the long as well as the short term, would-be motorcycle builders at the beginning of the century had little choice but to embrace the worthy principles of strength and simplicity. Apart from the obvious need to build something that would survive for more than a few minutes, there was precious little else in the way of foundations on which to build. The automotive industry in general was still in its nascent stage, with only minimal technological trickle-down to the even younger two-wheeled market. The best that an honest motorcycle maker could hope for was to acquire a reputation for reliability in a world scourged by appalling road surfaces and infested by fly-by-night shysters out for a quick buck.

That first Harley-Davidson was designed by chief engineer Bill Harley (the only college graduate among the founders), and built up by Walter Davidson, using patterns made by his brother Arthur. Though much effort was put into getting the machine up and running, an apocryphal tale still persists to the effect that this cycle was not immediately regarded by its creators as the progenitor of a long line of motorcycles intended for sale to the general public. Indeed, legend has it that the partners only began to see the commercial

possibilities when a mutual acquaintance asked them to build another 'Harley-Davidson' for his personal use.

Given the single-minded and concerted fashion in which the three men went about their task, with literally months of experimentation, fabrication and aggravation being capped by a not insignificant testing program on local roads, this admittedly attractive yarn is difficult to credit. The hard-headed approach displayed in later years by the company in regard to business matters tends to confirm the alternative that the founders knew exactly what they were doing all along. It is also a fact that both Bill Harley and Arthur Davidson were avid consumers of whatever information they could find within the covers of automotive and scientific journals. Harley in particular, with his level-headed attitude and better education, would certainly have been all too aware of the shortcomings of contemporary motorcycles and, by extension, of the yawning gap in the market that was so obviously waiting to be filled by a workmanlike and reliable offering.

The major problem with the first H-D machine was the fact that it was a compromise, designed and built as a motorised bicycle rather than as a true motorcycle. The drawbacks of this concept became all the more apparent when a more powerful, 25 cubic inch (420cc) version of the first engine was shoehorned into the by now severely overstressed frame. Still, the new motor proved to be a powerful and reliable enough base unit on which to build for the next three years, and was initially installed in H-D's first 'proper' motorcycle chassis which made its debut in the latter part of 1903.

Only one example of this, Harley-Davidson's first real motorcycle, was built. Although the original machine has long been lost to posterity, reconstructions still exist in museums. The most obvious advantages this revised model had over the prototype were in the area of wheelbase dimension (sensibly extended for better stability), and in the general beefing-up of the steering head and wheel bearings, the frame tubes, and the wheels. Final drive fol-

lowed the fashion of the day, being a leather belt which could be tightened or slackened by the rider in order to modulate the degree of grip on the large diameter rear sprocket (thereby altering the rate of forward progress).

The fuel tank hung from the crossbar, again an utterly conventional move. George Hendee's 1902 Indian, by contrast, featured a gas tank mounted in a novel position atop the rear fender. Throughout the fifty-year rivalry between H-D and Indian, the Milwaukee products would always be cast in the durable, slightly plodding role, while the Springfield machines had an altogether more glamorous and sporty image. The tortoise eventually triumphed over the hare, however, the 1953 demise of Indian bringing to an end that firm's glittering record of race wins and technological innovation.

Upon completion of the first 'real' Harley-Davidson, things suddenly began to happen. Over the winter of 1903-04, orders for two more models were fulfilled by the Davidsons, now operating out of a soon-to-be-enlarged 15ft by 10ft shed which had been erected by their father in his own back garden. Walter Davidson committed himself full-time to the fledgling business, and four more part-timers were taken on in early 1904 to help cope with the steadily increasing flow of orders. Bill Harley meanwhile had gone back to school to the University of Wisconsin in order to brush up on and redirect new engineering techniques back into the motorcycle's development process.

By 1905, production was up to eight machines a year, and even the extended shed was proving impossibly small. Once again, the Davidson family came to the rescue, the cost of a purpose-built factory site in Milwaukee being met by an uncle, James McLay. This was the turning point in H-D's history. From eight bikes in 1905, production shot up to 49 bikes in 1906, and tripled every year thereafter until 1910, at which point well over 3000 machines per annum were passing through what eventually became known as the Juneau Avenue works.

Below left: Ohio's 980cc Flying Merkel V-twins occasionally split the warring H-D and Indian racers in the 1910s. Braking systems were regarded by some as unmanly. . .

Right: . . .particularly on board racers like this H-D twin, where every pound shaved off the weight meant a little more speed. This example might be thought a trifle over-restored.

By this time, the only Davidson brother still remaining outside the family firm had also joined up. William A Davidson, the eldest of the three, had already acquired a reputation for hard but fair treatment of the men who had been working under him in his previous position as a foreman on the Chicago & Milwaukee Railroad. His new job at H-D of Vice President and Works Manager helped free up more of Arthur Davidson's time, allowing him to move into the increasingly vital area of sales promotion, where he spared no efforts in exploiting the public's hunger for mobility at a time when motor cars were still prohibitively expensive.

He was also able to make some capital out of the fact that Harley had concentrated on refining and improving the solitary model in their 'range', rather than taking the risky route attempted by some other manufacturers – often with disastrous results – of wholesale development and release of several models at one time. The inevitable consequence of such a shortsighted policy was that the image of motorcycling as a whole suffered, with riders often to be seen marooned at the side of the road, let down by poor quality machinery.

Not helping with this image problem was the inadequate silencing tacked onto many of the big single-cylinder bikes of the age. Here was one area in which Harley-Davidson had been especially careful, reasoning (again, quite rightly) that customers were more likely to be attracted by silence than scandal. If they wanted to soup up their machines later on by sawing a length off the exhaust pipe, well, that was their choice. But Harley-Davidsons would all chuff along quietly when they came out of the factory; that was the management's choice. As was the color, an inoffensive swathe of grey relieved only by the founders' names and the odd pinstripe, a scheme which gave rise to the H-D's popularly adopted sobriquet of 'The Silent Gray Fellow.' This nickname stuck with the factory for many years.

Despite the factory's efforts to promote its cycle as nothing more than a rugged and reliable mode of transport, many of the more intrepid owners were using these valuable attributes to good advantage in the excitingly new and challenging arena of motor sport. Although H-D did not actually frown on this practice, neither did they do anything to encourage it. The factory attitude to competition in general eventually evolved into a high state of mean-

spiritedness, and became the cause of much disgruntlement among those private racers who were expert enough to bring favorable publicity to the marque without so much as a cent's worth of works assistance.

Nonetheless, the company was not averse in the early days to putting its own products to the test. In 1908 Walter Davidson, who by this time had been appointed President and General Manager of the recently incorporated company (Bill Harley being the Chief Designer and Engineer, and Arthur Davidson the Secretary and General Sales Manager) decided to have a bash at the newly-formed Federation of American Motorcyclists' inaugural 'Endurance Run.' The route began at Catskill, New York, and took in Brooklyn, before finishing with a circumnavigation of Long Island. Plodding along in typically methodical style, Walter completed the course with a perfect score, beating 83 other riders on 21 other marques in the process. He then went on to take part in the FAM's Economy Run on the same machine, recording no less than 188mpg en route to victory.

The original 3 horsepower H-D had by then been on the streets for some six years. Bill Harley, returning from his successful spell at university, announced that it was time for an upgrade. By boring and stroking the motor to a new capacity of 35 cubic inches (around 575cc) and reinforcing the sprung front forks, Harley had his upgrade ready in time for a 1909 launch. It went under the model name of 5-35, reflecting the new horsepower rating as well as the piston displacement.

More significant by far, however, was Harley's other project, which involved the grafting onto the 5-35's crankcases of a second cylinder, at a 45 degree angle to the first. The V-twin idea was not a new one; the first Isle of Man TT race, held two years earlier in 1907, had been won very easily by Rem Fowler on a Peugeot-engined Norton employing this same format. Harley-Davidson had immediately noted the potential of such a layout, and had been tinkering with a mule engine of their own since Fowler's victory, but difficulties with the atmospheric inlet valve system had delayed the entry of a feasible production model.

By 1909, a solution had been reached with the fitment of mechanically activated valves – and the way was suddenly made clear for a whole new chapter to open up, not just for Harley-Davidson, but for motorcycling itself.

Expression
and Depression

The heart of any motorcycle is generally held to be its engine. Before the current era of fully-enclosed machines, it was always the art of motorcycle designers not just to integrate the power unit into the bike's overall styling, but to highlight it, draw attention to it, and turn it into a statement of the company's philosophy.

No manufacturer has succeeded so well in this totemisation game as Harley-Davidson. Harley equals V-twin; V-twin equals Harley: it's taken as read. Hardly surprising, considering the fact that V-twins have been exiting Milwaukee in an unbroken stream since 1909, first with the F and then in 1911 with the renowned J.

The appeal of the V-twin was clear enough in those early days. In exchange for a relatively small weight penalty, the single-cylinder engine's power capability could be increased by as much as 100 percent. In North America, with its vast travelling distances and thinly scattered law enforcement agencies, this feature alone was enough to convince motorcycle showroom browsers (many of whom were young and devil-may-care) that V-twins were the only way to go.

There was no shortage of choice in the market by the time Harley-Davidson moved into it. All the big domestic manufacturers – Indian, Excelsior, Flying Merkel – had at least one big 45 degree vee on their books, and all were doing well by them. There were disadvantages associated with this format, quite apart from the extra weight (which in any case was seen as a plus point by riders all too accustomed to being bounced out of the saddles of their lightweight singles).

The major negative was undoubtedly the V-twin's inherent vibration at higher engine speeds. By way of compensation, the excellent low-end performance more than made up for this shortcoming. With high gearing fitted to maximise the easy cruising properties of a luxuriant torque curve, the vibration could, to all intents and purposes, be relegated to the status of a minor annoyance.

With one cylinder lying directly behind the other, and hence out of the cooling airstream, the provision of copious finning on the cylinder barrels was even more critical on the V-twins than it had been on the singles. The practical effect of this was to restrict the potential for engine enlargement via the normal route of increasing the cylinder bores; there simply was not sufficient room between the pots to expand in that direction. Instead, significant capacity increases could only be gained by the more involved method of lengthening the stroke, a technique which certainly resulted in even better bottom end response, but only at the expense of a rather limited ability to rev out at the top end. Almost all of the American companies quickly came to the conclusion that the best compromise between smoothness and power in a V-twin was to be had in an engine capacity of 61 cubic inches (1000cc) – a size which remains popular for V-twins even now.

Previous page: The J model was perhaps Harley's best-liked. Its 18-year production run ended in 1929.

Right: A closer look at the J's 61 cubic inch (1000cc) engine, here shown in a 1915 model. The classic 45-degree angle between the cylinders is still a major feature of Harleys going into the 1990s.

Below: A 1920 advertisement for the J from Britain's *Motor Cycle* magazine.

Left: Smooth-running four cylinder machines like this 1914 Henderson posed a threat to Harley's vibey twins, but H-D chose not to respond with a four of their own.

Going into the second decade of the century, the mushrooming popularity of competitive motorcycle sport, particularly on the new board tracks and dirt ovals, underlined the timeliness of H-D's move into big twins. Not that the factory officially approved of this trend, of course; at least, not if sponsorship was being requested. Their support remained confined to the more sedate world of reliability trials and the like, highlighting with some justification the less overtly sporting strengths of their motorcycle.

Number one rivals Indian, meanwhile, were profiting from H-D's reticence, enjoying success after success on racetracks around the world. Events in 1911 were symptomatic of the two firms' different attitudes. While Indian were sweeping the board at the Isle of Man Tourist Trophy races in June, the feathered headdress emblems shining proudly on the fuel tanks of the first three machines home, Harley-Davidson were busy putting the finishing touches to a primitive 'idler' mechanism, designed to allow manual disconnection of the drive to the rear wheel at temporary halts.

Although H-D were publicly criticised by dealers and racers alike for what was seen as their unenterprising and poor-spirited policy of non-involvement in racing, the fact of the matter was that H-D's ordinary street machines were – like every other manufacturer's, if they were honest enough to admit it – in sore need of basic development. Advances like the idler mechanism were of direct benefit to the ordinary H-D rider, who up to that point had been obliged to pedal-restart his machine after all but the very briefest of stops.

Nonetheless, the factory's view that a dollar spent on research and development in the workshop was better than a dollar spent on funding the antics of a bunch of speed-crazy fools, was one that was destined to change, in spite of the unyielding dogmatism which was being displayed by H-D's founders at this time.

More useful advances were made in 1912, particularly in the transmission department. The inclusion in the specification of a multiplate clutch allowed the factory to replace the 8E V-twin's unreliable old leather belt (which nevertheless continued to appear on the single until 1914) with a far more trustworthy chain.

Below: A classic Indian V-twin from 1920. George Hendee's machines were always quicker and more sophisticated than the equivalent Harley models, but in the end it was the Milwaukee firm which had enough stamina to survive.

Meantime, the Milwaukee factory was continually growing to keep pace with the public's apparently insatiable demand for cheap transport. Sidecars were particularly popular. By 1912, annual production was up to more than 10,000 machines, and Arthur Davidson's unstinting efforts to build up a comprehensive dealer network were beginning to bear fruit, with Harleys becoming increasingly common on roads in the more remote parts of the United States.

Inevitably, booming sales of street bikes only served to stimulate still further the activity on the nation's racetracks. Harley-Davidson's detached stance in this area was becoming more and more inappropriate; so much so that in 1913 the founders were finally forced to accept the need for change. They engaged the services of William Ottaway, ostensibly as Assistant Engineer under Bill Harley, but in reality as the head of a newly created racing department.

Ottaway's credentials were impeccable. Up to that time he had been responsible for the production of the highly competitive 'White Thor' racers for the rival Thor Motorcycles group. His new brief at Milwaukee was to extract more power from H-D's existing engines, while Bill Harley addressed the long overdue matter of designing the two-speed gearbox that would be essential for racing. Ottaway quickly vindicated the founders' decision to hire him, not only by bumping up the 1000cc V-twin's power output, but also by putting together an all-new, limited edition competition bike – the 11K. This machine, incorporating all of Ottaway's tuning modifications in a purpose built light-

weight chassis, went on to thrust Harley-Davidson straight into the forefront of motorcycle racing – quite a jump for a company which had up to that point shown no interest in such frippery.

The 11K almost made a sensational debut at the inaugural 300 Mile Classic race on Dodge City's two-mile track in July 1914, H-D's works rider Walter Cunningham storming into the lead at the 100-mile point ahead of well-established riders on rather more distinguished machinery. Glen Boyd prevented the upset by taking the chequered flag on one of George Hendee's all-conquering eight-valve Indians, but only after Cunningham had been sidelined by chain and spark plug problems while still in the lead. The well-drilled Harley teamsters continued to show good form in the remaining 1914 season races, doing everything bar actually winning. That pleasure would have to wait until 1915, a year which marked the start of a long spell of success by the works 'Wrecking Crew' team, sweeping all before them on Ottaway-designed eight-valve versions of the 11K racer.

It was a shame that H-D's overdue blossoming as a performance-orientated motorcycle company coincided with two epochal events which shaped the destinies of ordinary people all over the world. Despite its name, the first of these events – the World War – in some ways had less direct effect on the American people than did the second, which was full implementation of production line techniques by the automobile manufacturer Henry Ford. Almost overnight, motor cars became affordable for the common man; at the same time, warning bells began to sound for those motorcycle manufacturers

Top: Harleys were used extensively by the American forces of law and order, often because they were somewhat cheaper than rival machinery. This is a typical 1916 squad.

Left: In the same year, the US Expeditionary Force found a use for Harleys in Mexico, for the pursuit of famed bandit Pancho Villa.

Right: One of Milwaukee's less popular releases, the fore-and-aft 584cc 'W' flat twin, which ran from 1919 to 1922.

Left: Though the 'W' Sport Twin was a reasonable attempt at cashing in on a format which was popular in Europe, it proved too unexciting for the power-hungry USA market.

Right: Harley's big Milwaukee plant on Juneau Avenue, seen here in the latter part of the 1920s, was the subject of many expansion programs after its humble start in 1906.

Below right: Claude Temple enjoyed many successes on H-Ds outside of his own career as a motorcycle manufacturer. He won this 1921 Brooklands race at an average speed of 92.37mph.

whose prosperity had been founded on the relative cheapness of their products. The gradual weeding-out process affecting the weaker American marques gathered pace as war conditions severely restricted the importation from Europe of ancillary items not then produced by the native industry.

Indian, at that time the biggest motorcycle firm in America, suffered greatly in the war from self-inflicted wounds caused by the commitment of too great a proportion of their total output to military motorcycle production. In keeping with their conservative traditions, Harley-Davidson adopted a more circumspect posture. By offering a much smaller portion of their output to the government, they were able to maintain a healthy home market. Indeed, by exploiting Indian's short-sightedness, H-D were able to expand their agency network by poaching many of the Springfield company's under-supplied and understandably disaffected dealers.

When the war ended in 1918, Indian's home market had been effectively plundered. Harley-Davidson had improved their own position relative to Indian, such that the two companies were now very much on an equal footing with around 1000 dealers each. Detecting a bright future ahead, H-D's founders authorised another factory expansion programme in readiness for what they expected to be a doubling up of production from their sub-20,000 annual output during the straitened war years.

To take maximum advantage of the new trading conditions, the faithful old Model 9 single, the 'Silent Gray Fellow', was discontinued in 1918, to be replaced in 1919 by a totally new model. The horizontally-opposed 37 cubic inch (600cc) Model W 'Sport Twin' was a Douglas lookalike, aimed squarely at Indian's highly rated Scout lightweight.

Unfortunately, and not for the last time, the market had been misjudged by Harley-Davidson. American motorcyclists were still in love with the big, fast 'Model J' V-twin. The Sport Twin was not what they wanted at that time, being rather slow and uninspiring. It sold reasonably well in H-D's recently created European export market, its abstemious consumption of fuel being perfectly suited to the depressed post-war conditions, but the home market dictated its early demise in 1922 – a year which turned out to be one of the worst in the American motorcycle industry's short history.

As the 1920s began, Henry Ford's master plan to swamp the country in a tidal wave of black Model Ts was already well advanced. Waking up to the threat, the other big players in the US auto industry launched a counterwave of competing econo-cars. This was all very bad news for the bike firms, whose fortunes immediately nosedived as precipitously as Ford's had soared. The problem was that the role of motorcycling had suddenly

changed from that of essential transport provider into a far less crucial one based on leisure. The sea-change was partly attributable to the bike manufacturers' own realignment towards competition in the mid-1910s. Many of Harley-Davidson's older and wiser employees predictably saw this as a belated vindication of Harley's much-criticised pre-war position on non-involvement. Nobody had foreseen the threat from Ford, nor the transformation it wreaked on the world of transport; accordingly, nobody had made any plans to reposition the motorcycle in the marketplace.

Ironically enough, Harley-Davidson's race team were by this stage breaking records at board and oval meetings all over the country, including the posting of the first ever 100mph-plus team victory at the Fresno, California track in early 1921. The 'Crew' also won the fifth Dodge City 300 Mile event in that same year. But the parlous economic conditions, combined with the futility (and expense) of attempting national domination over the still-strong Indian and Excelsior-mounted opposition, finally forced H-D to pull out of racing altogether at the end of 1921. The announcement was made by President Davidson in a circular release to Harley dealers: 'We find that we have become engaged in two distinct businesses at the factory; one, the business of racing, with a complete separate organisation, and the other, the legitimate business of making and selling motorcycles.'

A ruthless program of cost-cutting came into immediate effect, not just in the racing department, whose staff were literally disowned in the middle of a race meeting, but right throughout the entire company. If H-D were badly off, Indian were in a terrible state, their 1920 production figure of 20,000 being slashed to less than 7000 the following year. Both firms somehow staggered through to 1922, albeit in a severely trimmed state.

To avoid further blood-letting, a truce was arranged between the two companies. Over lunch in New York's Astor Hotel, Arthur Davidson and Indian's general manager Frank Weschler agreed to standardise the prices of competing models, so as to kill off the potentially ruinous effects of price-cutting. Nowadays, such an arrangement would, if uncovered, be vilified under the heading of cartel price-fixing; in 1922, it was the natural solution to a simple problem, and one which allowed both parties to make sensible plans for the future without having to keep looking over each other's shoulders. These price-fixing meetings went on to become an indispensable annual appointment for the managers of Indian and Harley-Davidson.

Having established the rules of the game in the most gentlemanly fashion, the two motorcycling giants then went away to lay plans for each other's destruction. For their part, Harley-Davidson's sales strategy was based on the

Left: Legendary British ace Freddie Dixon had good cause to grin after yet another win (this time at the 1923 Clipstone Speed Trials) on his modded JD racer.

Right: Douglas Davidson (no relation), here pictured at Brooklands in July 1921, had achieved a place in the record books one year earlier by becoming the first British rider to top 100mph.

Below right: Freddie Dixon again, making one schoolboy's dream come true in 1921.

launch of the JD, a larger-engined version of the faithful 1000cc J V-twin. Although the 1200cc JD was primarily aimed at the heavy duty three-wheeler commercial market, which still persisted despite the car-induced demolition of the private sidecar market, the new motor's extra power struck a sympathetic chord among the new breed of enthusiast motorcyclists moving in to fill the vacuum left behind by the Model T defectors. In this connection, the '74' (the JD's capacity in cubic inches) was also a useful response to the Chief, Indian's highly capable and well-favored entry in the heavyweight stakes. Looking back, the 74 could certainly be deemed a success, as this engine size and type featured in the Harley-Davidson lineup right up to 1980, and thereafter (in Sporster format) until the present day.

Following the success of their talks the previous year, Arthur and Walter Davidson arranged another meeting with Indian's Frank Weschler in 1923. The subject this time was the ejection from H-D and Indian sales showrooms of all other motorcycling marques, such as Excelsior, Cleveland and Reading Standard. Although Weschler was reportedly less than keen on this idea, having enjoyed the benefits of business cooperation and personal friendships with the representatives of these 'second division' companies for many years, the Davidsons finally prevailed upon him to agree to their proposal. The aim was to establish true solus franchises; the human consequence of this ruthless scheme was, inevitably, the demise of many smaller makes.

Another consequence of this pact was the creation of conditions suitable for a consolidation of Harley-Davidson's position at home, in Europe, and even Japan, where they established a foothold to challenge Indian's already firmly rooted Tokyo-based operation. This Japanese connection would eventually result in the setting up of a Harley-producing subsidiary in the Ginza district, which was in fact the first motorcycle manufacturing plant in Japan. Given the state of enmity which now exists between Harley riders and the Japanese 'opposition,' it is extraordinary and not a little ironic to think that the first motorcycles to be built on a commercial basis in Japan were Harley-Davidsons sold under the Rikuo badge.

In the mid-1920s, the transportation demands of America's forces of law and order were such that firms could make a healthy contribution to their own balance sheets by securing contracts to supply police motorcycles. The vibration problem that was an inbuilt design fault of big V-twins led many police officers to prevail upon their employers to let them use the much

smoother four-cylinder offerings of Henderson and Ace. The 1924 disappearance of Ace from the motorcycling scene cut down the choice somewhat, and naturally aroused the interest of Harley-Davidson, who could see big potential sales in the offing for any firm willing to put up a viable alternative to the Henderson.

Recognising that they did not possess the in-house expertise to produce an all-new engine, H-D immediately employed Ace's now redundant chief design engineer, Everett DeLong, on a brief to come up with a cheap new four-cylinder unit. Working in secret, DeLong quickly penned what he and the few others who were privy to the project considered to be a commercially worthy design. Effectively two sleeved-down J 74 twins laid side by side, the DeLong motor seemed to meet H-D's criteria. Bill Davidson, however, was not convinced; using his power as the company's leading shareholder, he vetoed the project on the grounds that it would have been too expensive to produce. Shortly afterwards, DeLong left the company to work for Cleveland, and all traces of the stillborn four-cylinder Harley-Davidson were destroyed.

The founders thus had to content themselves with a simple cosmetic revamping of the justly popular but by then old-fashioned J. Their options were necessarily limited by the fact that the J was their only high-profile model throughout the period of 1922-1929, after the Sport Twin's extinction in 1922 and before the arrival of the 45 cubic inch (750cc) model D in 1929. The improvements made to the J included a few welcome modifications to the engine, specifically to the valvegear and lubrication system, which were enough to ensure continuing loyalty among the 74's large and devoted band of followers.

Another continuing trend, and a somewhat less pleasant topic for discussion at H-D board meetings, was the apparently inexorable waning of motorcycling's popularity in the mid 1920s. Harley-Davidson were obliged to move into the ancillary parts business because of the fact that so many of their suppliers were being forced into closure by the prevailing economic circumstances. Their total output of machines was running at pre-war levels, only around 12,000 bikes being built in 1924. Even so, that made Harley-Davidson the biggest American manufacturer, with Indian producing approximately half as many machines as H-D. The only other manufacturer of note, Excelsior, was running at about half Indian's capacity, relying heavily on its police sales of Henderson fours.

Left: Harleys were designed to run best on America's ultra straight freeways, but that didn't stop this 1920's group from tackling the crookedest street in San Francisco.

Right: From 1922, the 1000cc 'J' had a big brother, the 1200cc 'JD'. Gray had turned to olive by then too.

Below: The 350cc Peashooter, available in both side valve and ohv formats, was campaigned on American tracks to great effect by Joe Petrali.

In 1925, Indian and Cleveland attempted to revitalise their flagging fortunes by launching lightweight single-cylinder bikes of 21 cubic inch (350cc) capacity. This engine size was extremely popular in England, home of the world's biggest motorcycle market at that time, so the American firms' decision to try and break into that field was a logical one. Equally predictable was Harley-Davidson's response the following year, in the shape of two separate 350cc singles. Model A was a sidevalve plodder capable of around 50mph (assuming that the piston could be persuaded to hold together at such a giddy speed). Model B differed in that it featured overhead valvegear, which endowed it with a considerably higher and more reliably obtainable top end of around 65mph.

The Harley dealership network, bred on a steady diet of fast V-twins, was less than enthusiastic about the new singles. But, after cynically dubbing the bikes 'Peashooters,' the same dealers were later required to eat their words. Although sales success was not instant in the US, where riders were not especially bothered about the 350's economy (its most obvious selling point), its race successes in the national series specially created for this class

Previous page: A long-track specification overhead valve Harley racer of the Great War period.

Left: Swedish daredevil Erik Westerberg did 104mph on his Harley on the ice of Stockholm's Edsviken Bay – without studs or spikes. . .

Below: Speedway was a popular sport in England in the late 1920s. Harley's Peashooter variant (foreground) had its work cut out against BSAs like the background example.

Right: Motorcycle sport of all kinds was incredibly well supported in the 1920s. This hillclimbing Harley sidecar entry looks like a family affair.

of machine were more difficult to ignore. The heroic feats of Joe Petrali on America's new 'flat track' circuits and on the notorious 'widowmaker' hill climbs were to assure him of a position of honor in the annals of Peashooter and, indeed, Harley-Davidson history.

Pressing home their advantage, H-D delighted their big twin fans with the announcement in 1927 of the JH (61ci) and JD-H (74ci) variants, scheduled for production in 1928. The most notable and attractive feature of these new roadburners was the utilisation of twin camshafts to operate the valves. Although aimed at the very top end of the market, with a suitably lofty price ticket nearly 20 percent higher than that of the ordinary J, the twin cammers were sufficiently impressive machines to earn themselves the reputation as

the best Harleys ever made. It was unfortunate that the factory chose to wait so long before indulging itself in such a commendable upgrading exercise, since the worthy but venerable J was by this time fast reaching the end of its run.

There was about to be a major shakeup in the Harley range, in fact, with the launch of two new models in 1929 and 1930. The first new model was destined to underwrite the company's future for the next twenty years; the second one nearly damaged the company's reputation beyond repair.

And in between the two launches, events on Wall Street threatened to bring about the ruin not just of Harley-Davidson, but of every other company, corporation and conglomerate in the industrialised world.

Indian Troubles

At the close of the last chapter, mention was made of Harley-Davidson's launch of two new models at the end of the 1920s.

In fact, *three* machines were announced by the factory in 1929, but only two of these were to play a significiant role in the company's history. More-over, two of these three machines were all but identical, and hence could almost be classified as one model – though this was far from being the image the factory was trying to portray. At a casual glance, these two machines were practically indistinguishable from one another. The fact that one was powered by a 500cc single, and the other by a 750cc V-twin, was indicative of the extraordinary simplistic thinking behind Harley-Davidson's model range policy at this time.

With or without hindsight, it now seems astonishing that any motorcycle company could simultaneously offer such an ill-considered pair of models as the 45 cubic inch (750cc) D V-twin and the 30.5 cubic inch (500cc) C single for sale to the general public. In this case, not for the first time, Harley-Davidson's almost fanatical concern with keeping costs down nearly led to their undoing.

The notion this time was, quite simply, a brazen attempt to make two motorcycles out of one. The 750cc D started off badly by being encumbered with a torquey but over-lazy and decidedly underpowered sidevalve motor. While contemporary equivalents from Indian and Excelsior were easily cap-able of speeds approaching 80mph, Harley's supposedly competitive 45 could not even touch 60mph. Worse yet, it had a nasty tendency to destroy itself if the frustrated rider decided to fly in the face of reason by attempting to keep up with the rapidly-departing opposition.

Other compromises had had to be built into the D, for no other reason than that H-D had wanted to make use of exactly the same frame and cycle parts for the C. Of necessity, these frame components had to be beefy enough to contain the bigger and more powerful engine of the two. The inevitable consequence was that the C's rather feeble 500cc single motor had a decidedly hard job pushing the excess weight of a 750cc-sized chassis along the road. The whole ill-conceived exercise was a classic example of over-rationalisation, a felony which was then compounded by inadequate development.

The only saving grace on either machine was the provision of a front brake, a feature which, somewhat incredibly, had made its first appearance on Harleys only one year earlier on the 61 and 74 cubic inch V-twins. Even then, it had been regarded with some skepticism by those who thought of themselves as true Milwaukee men. These riders considered front brakes to be abominations and the work of the devil. In a curious way, applying this idea to Harley-Davidsons in isolation, they were half right.

Previous page: A beautifully kept 1936 61-E Knucklehead.

Right: The tough WLA army bike gave sterling service in the testing conditions of World War II, where the Harley's reliability and ease of servicing were of key significance. Some 89,000 were produced.

Below: The wheel has come full circle, with H-D now offering a springer-forked model for the '90s, but this is an original springer, with gold-plated custom touches.

With the notable exception of the XLCR Cafe Racer in 1977, Harley-Davidsons for the street have always been designed along cruising rather than racing lines. As such, they have traditionally featured riding positions which require the rider to maintain a straight back and forward-extended limbs, in a posture not too dissimilar to that assumed when driving a car. Such a posture has the effect of biasing the overall weight distribution towards the rear of the cycle, which in turn permits enthusiastic use of the back brake without too much risk of wheel lockup. Even today, a certain degree of care is advisable when using H-D front brakes, particularly on models featuring skinny 'custom' front tyres. The distrust of Harley's 1928 customers (riding on somewhat less tenacious rubber) was, therefore, not wholly unjustified.

In the event, buyers of the 1929 D and C sidevalve models had other things to worry about, thanks to the factory's failure to put either model through a serious development program. The nature of the shared frame meant that, while there was no problem fitting the single-pot C motor, serious difficulties were encountered when it came to shoe-horning in the much bigger twin. Although the basic engine went in all right, there was insufficient clearance for the 45's generator to be sited in its usual V-twin location, ahead of the crankcase. Instead, provision had to be made for it to be fitted slightly ahead and to the left of the vee made by the cylinders. From a distance, bystanders observing the passage of a D mistook the large cylindrical generator for an extra cylinder; the unsurprising result was that the D quickly acquired a 'three-cylinder Harley' misnomer.

It took even less time for this unfortunate machine to acquire a hatful of less innocent nicknames, bestowed upon it by angry dealers and their customers once it had become obvious that the generator's botched-up bevel gear drive was not strong enough to hold together under pressure. Worse still, the clutch components (which were already in service on the small capacity A and B singles, as well as on the new C model) were plainly inadequate for use in a motor twice the size − even if it was almost certainly less than twice as powerful. Harley-Davidson were not inclined to release horsepower figures at this time, probably with good reason in the 45's case.

Besieged by complaints, the factory hurriedly revamped the D, fitting

bigger bearings in the generator drive and, in an attempt to rectify the performance shortcomings, including a larger bore carburetor in the specification. This modification hauled the 45's top speed over the 60mph mark, hardly an earth-shattering tune-up but a step in the right direction at least. The new 'performance' image was further enhanced by a quick restyle of the fuel and oil tanks. Despite all its initial teething problems, the 45 eventually became the backbone of Harley's model range, continuing in production as the power unit for solo mounts until 1953, and in the role of commercial slave in Harley's three-wheel Servicars right up until 1974.

The C proved rather less resilient. America's predilection for big-inch cruisers had already been firmly established long before the end of the 1920s. The much smaller market for European-style singles was by definition more difficult to satisfy, but having opted to compete in that market, H-D's approach was then inexplicably casual.

There was sales resistance even before the C was launched. The so-called 'Baby Harley' was far from being a worthy example of the sports single genre, combining as it did the twin failings of unexciting performance and unremarkable reliability. When it was unveiled, weighing in at a hefty 365 pounds, it seemed that the motorcycling public's advance appraisal of the machine was uncomfortably accurate. Like the D, it was hard pushed to reach the 60mph claimed for it by its manufacturers; also like the D, it proved itself to be fragile right out of the crate. Cooling was its weakness. The piston displaying an alarming propensity to eat itself in the hands of anyone who felt inclined to test its open-throttle behavior.

By 1931, the Baby Harley had lost its relatively lightweight Model B-derived frame, in favor of the 45's by then revised chassis. In the process, the C gained over 60 pounds and became even more sluggish than before. Though it did not officially disappear from the H-D catalog until 1937 (thanks in large part to its popularity as a commercial hauler in Japan of all places), sales in the USA had never been anything other than desultory.

If the C was bad, then the all-new 74 cubic inch V-twin revealed in August 1929 was a disaster. While Harley-Davidson's strong following might have allowed them to commit one *faux pas* in what was for them an unfamiliar market in small singles, a similar failure in their own specialist niche of

Left: The 'Twin Cam' JD and JDH big twins were only produced for a short time at the end of the 1920s, but were an instant hit with sports-minded riders.

Right: Charles Lindbergh, the first man to fly the Atlantic, was an enthusiastic Harley man in his spare time.

Below: The 45 cubic inch DLD of 1929 was known as 'the three-cylinder Harley' because of its unusual generator placement, but this more modern mutant (spotted at Daytona) really does have three cylinders.

V-twins – coming so soon after the 45's inauspicious debut – should have been unthinkable.

And yet, unbelievably, it appeared that the company had not learned its lesson. The new VL, put forward as the long-overdue replacement for the 15-year-old J, was a 74 cubic inch (1200cc) lookalike of the 45ci D. With a new frame and stronger forks, it was nearly 25 percent heavier than the J at around 550 pounds fully wet, and offered little in the way of innovation, other than quickly-detachable wheels and the option of a more contemporary style of sidecar. In fact, the main 'advance' claimed by the factory was not an advance at all, but simply a retention of existing sidevalve technology. The most often-quoted benefit was that maintenance would be made easier by dint of the fact that the engine could be left in the frame during routine top-

end work. Retention of the total-loss lubrication system was further evidence of the VL's conservative specification.

On the face of it, the VL did not look like the kind of machine that might upset H-D's traditionally conservative clientele. Quality of construction had never been a problem at Milwaukee, and the VL was no exception to that rule. The bike's deficiencies were as much conceptual as mechanical.

Ricardo-designed heads, in conjunction with unusually small flywheels, were intended to pep up the engine's performance. These flywheels certainly enhanced the bike's low-speed pickup and accelerative qualities, but only at the cost of severely diminished top-end power. The VL's output turned out to be no greater than that of the J, and such power as it did have seemed to vanish altogether at higher engine speeds, a disappearing trick signalled all

Right: The 74 cubic inch VL sidevalve twin did not represent much of a step forward for Harley-Davidson. It was discontinued in 1936.

Below: Harleys have always been very popular in Japan. In fact, the first recorded importation took place as early as 1912. The three-wheeled Servicar derivative found especial favor in crowded Tokyo.

too painfully by the coincident commencement of serious vibration. The fly-wheels were too small, a fact pointedly brought to the factory's attention by disappointed dealers and owners worldwide. Once again, Harley-Davidson had released a machine for public consumption without having put it through any sort of serious test program.

New crankcases incorporating bigger flywheels were hastily fabricated and shipped out to H-D dealers, along with newly enlarged frames, with the instruction that these items should be retro-fitted to all VLs either sold or still on the showroom floor – a total of over 1300 cycles. Power-increasing alterations to the camshaft and valves were handed down at the same time. No financial assistance was offered to the dealers to help them in this massive clean-up operation, with the result that more than a few tore up their Harley franchises in protest. Other dealers who pleaded with the company to put the much-loved J back into production were also disappointed by H-D's negative response.

Additional pressure was put on the already struggling dealer network in 1929 as a result of a misguided decision by America's newly-elected President Hoover to erect import barriers in order to protect the nation's farmers from the ruinous effects of cheap imports and rising inflation at home. Faced with the prospect of having to negotiate Hoover's tariff hurdles, foreign governments predictably retaliated by hoisting import barriers of their own. America's exporting potential was strangled at a stroke, obliging companies like Harley-Davidson to streamline their home marketing in order to survive. Dealers were whipped into action in search of turnover in the civilian and (increasingly important) police sales areas, competing furiously against Indian and Excelsior/Henderson.

The extra effort looked like it might pay off, with signs of a slight upturn in the domestic motorcycle market despite the launch fiascos perpetrated by Harley-Davidson. But then, in October 1929, came the stock market crash on Wall Street. Suddenly there was unemployment on a massive scale as first banks and then businesses went under. The value of transportation fell through the floor as Americans across the country found themselves struggling to stay alive. Gasoline became a luxury item. Cars became next to worthless. Sales of motorcycles, at the bottom of the heap, began a downward slide which was to bottom out for Harley-Davidson in 1933, when just over 3300 units were sold – only slightly above the equivalent figure for 1910.

H-D's founders were in no position materially to assist their rapidly-shrinking dealers. All they could do was encourage them to greater efforts in the fight to take as big a proportion as possible of whatever market remained open to them. That effectively meant squeezing out their main competitor, Indian. Going into 1930, this was a prospect which seemed on the cards, as the Springfield company had been slowly bleeding to death for years at the hands of successive incompetent managers.

But in April of 1930, Harley-Davidson's plans received a setback when the fabulously wealthy industrialist E. Paul du Pont bought a majority stake in Indian, announcing at the same time his intention to ensure the firm's continuing involvement in the production of motorcycles. Excelsior, meanwhile, were capitalising on Harley's discomfiture over the VL (which had led to the cancellation of many police force orders), increasing production of their own Hendersons to fill the gap. Fortunately for H-D, however, this additional threat to their position was dissipated almost immediately by Excelsior themselves with their suicidal decision to fit cheaper – and considerably less reliable – ignition systems to their police-specification machines. An important order by the Californian Highway Patrol was botched by Excelsior as a result, and marked the beginning of their withdrawal from the motorcycle industry.

It was now a straight fight between Harley-Davidson and Indian for control of the American market. H-D had their gloves off right from the start, outraging motorcyclists nationwide with a scheme which encouraged their dealers to scrap any non-Harleys which were brought into their shops as part-exchanges for (very attractively priced) VL police specials. This dubious policy had the effect of decimating the number of Indians on the road, and lifted the state of rivalry between the two firms to such a pitch that ordinary civilian riders of Harleys were turned away from Indian dealerships, and vice versa. So much rancour was caused that even the ruthless H-D management felt morally obliged to discontinue the offer, dropping it six months after its introduction.

Great damage had been done to the public images of both manufacturers

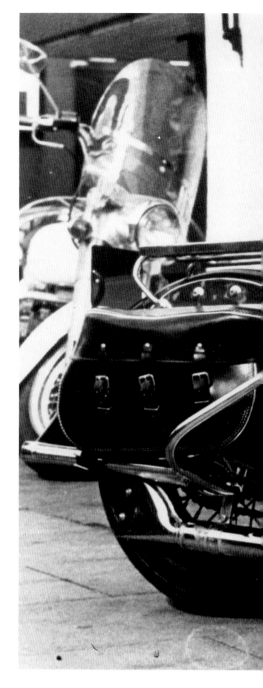

One of Harley's longest-lived and most successful models was the sidevalve '45', a docile plodder in the best H-D tradition. Thousands of 45s are still in use today; this one has been the subject of much tender loving care.

by then. Nonetheless, the annual price-fixing conferences between H-D and Indian continued to take place. The cosiness of the 1932 meeting was disturbed by the surprise attendance of E. Paul du Pont, who took the opportunity to lecture the Davidson brothers Walter (President) and Arthur (Sales Manager) on the subject of business ethics in general. Du Pont was especially caustic on the subject of H-D's seeming duplicity in the case of the VL police bikes deal, the details of which had of course not been divulged to Indian's representative at previous meetings.

Recovering from their initial shock at du Pont's outburst, the Davidson's calmed a potentially explosive situation by apologising to the French-born industrialist, and citing the need for desperate measures in a desperate situation. By this time, the 45 had been revamped, with a new frame (which allowed the troublesome generator to be sited in its proper place, ahead of the front cylinder) and a new purpose-built transmission. The 74ci VL had also benefitted from the upgrading of its previously suspect clutch. By 1932, both twins had secured a measure of public trust. They may not have been the world's most exciting motorcycles, but at least they were reasonably reliable.

This image of Harley-Davidsons as rather prosaic, functional motorcycles seems at odds with the marque's currently glamorous profile, but the reputation of the Milwaukee products was undoubtedly built on humble foundations. The Servi-car, launched in 1932, exemplified this practical aspect. Although this curious looking three-wheeled contraption has strong Harley associations, Indian had actually pre-empted H-D in the States with their own three-wheeler, the 'Dispatch-Tow', a device whose purpose was to facilitate the delivery of motor cars to and from garages by providing transport for the driver before and after such deliveries (the Dispatch-Tow being hitched behind the car).

The Servi-car/Dispatch-Tow format had already been a common sight on Japanese roads for some time before the Indian appeared, in the shape of H-D single-powered commercial 'rear cars'. In the States, the Servi-car soon found a niche as a light-duty delivery vehicle, and also as a means of transport for parking penalty officers. Because of the easy starting capability of the D 45ci engine, motorcycling experience was not a necessary prerequisite for would-be meter attendants; indeed, many of them were women.

By 1933, Harley-Davidson's model lineup was beginning to look quite respectable, although Indian's competing machinery was still dynamically superior in most respects. It was a pity that the full effects of the national recession were biting at their hardest at this time. Motorcycle production was troughing out, and racetrack activity had just about ground to a halt. In a desperate attempt to inject some life back into the sport, the American Motorcyle Association instigated a new racing framework.

The most significant feature of the new setup was the formation of Class C racing, aimed primarily at private riders on 45 cubic inch motorcycles. Harley-Davidson were initially not displeased by this turn of events, since it would pitch their revamped 45 against Indian's discontinued – but still fast – 101 Scout 750. Their confidence was to be undermined in 1935, however, by the reappearance of a new and still better Scout. Only through the expert ministrations of ace tuner Tom Sifton were H-D able to keep their 45 in the running for honors against the lighter and more maneuverable Indians.

Through a quirk in the rules, Class C also allowed overhead valve 500cc machines to compete. This provision had little immediate impact, but it would ultimately lead to friction within the American motorcycle industry with the arrival from England of Norton's astonishingly successful International. Harley's own 21 and 30.5ci singles were coincidentally withdrawn

from the home market in 1934, the factory having accepted that their future lay in big, powerful V-twins. Four-stroke singles would not resurface in the model range until 1961.

At the other end of H-D's product line-up, the 74ci VL was maturing into the kind of motorcycle which would reaffirm the public's faith in Harleys as solid and reliable mounts. For the 1936 model year, it was bored out to 80 cubic inches (1340cc), not to make it any quicker especially, but to endow it with even more lugging power for commercial and sidecar applications. An optional transmission with three forward gears and a reverse was included in the catalog with these duties in mind. The new 80 (factory designation VLH) displayed an advanced tendency to vibrate and/or overheat – sometimes to the point of seizure – if it was subjected to extended hard use, but other than that it was a workmanlike machine with much to recommend it over Indian's now slower and often cantankerous Chief.

H-D widened the appeal of their cycles in the mid-1930s with the invention of the 'buddy seat', a foreshortened dual seat which allowed the Harley man to take his girl for an outing. The outing would for preference be short, however, or the girl of a very friendly disposition, since a buddy seat placed the two riders in very close contact with one another. One is forced to the conclusion that there are indeed many friendly girls in the US, since the buddy-style seat (admittedly rather more spacious now) still figures on modern-day Harleys.

1936 was one of the most important years in Harley-Davidson's history, ushering in as it did a new age of overhead valve V-twins. First in what was to become a 16-year line of highly-regarded ohv machinery was the 61 cubic inch (1000cc) model E, an all-new, 36 horsepower, duplex framed blockbuster aimed squarely at the sporting rider. As the 61E gradually moved into Harley-Davidson's hall of fame, its distinctively shaped rocker covers eventu-

ally gave rise to the 'knucklehead' sobriquet used to describe this type of engine. The regard in which this motor came to be held may be measured by the fact that it is still one of the most prized powerplants among America's outlaw and custom fraternities, even though the last factory unit was built in 1952.

And yet, once again, the fate of a new Harley was almost sealed before it had had a chance to make a favorable impact, thanks once more to the factory's indecent haste in rushing into production before adequate testing had been carried out. In the manufacturer's defense, they did allow William Harley's son William J to put in some development miles on two 61E prototypes. But, having done so, they then refused to take cognisance of the faults which were brought to light by this testing.

The most serious shortcoming was in the ohv arrangement itself, which showed itself capable of leaking large quantities of oil. Ignoring all advice concerning the importance of getting it right first time with his ohv debutant, President Walter Davidson insisted on sticking to the June 1936 launch date. No delays could be contemplated.

The results were predictable – and disastrous.

All pictures: The 61-E 'Knucklehead' of 1936 was a watershed machine in Harley's history. The first overhead valve big twin, this engine is effectively the father of all models currently on sale. Gears were selected by hand via the tank-mounted lever. Production ceased in 1952, but the knucklehead motor is still very much sought after as a basis for one-off specials.

Knuckleheads
and Panheads

The 61E of 1936 was a pivotal machine in Harley-Davidson's often troubled history. As their first overhead valve V-twin, the 'Knucklehead' led the way forward into a fifty-year dynasty of overhead valve-engined motorcycles which now shows every sign of propagating itself right into the 21st century.

Looking back at the E's launch, however, it is all too easy to imagine a very different set of consequences which, if they had been allowed to happen, and given the teetering state of H-D's economic position at the time, might well have jeopardised the existence of the company itself. Only the dogged resilience of the founders – coupled with their already well-known firmness with dealers – saved the Knucklehead from sudden and ignominious death.

It was not long after the release of the 61E before the inadequacy of the new bike's valvegear was discovered by dealers and customers. Public confi-

dence in the factory's ability to produce reliable machinery, already dented earlier by the equally unimpressive debuts of the 45 and 74ci VLs, took another severe knock. The feeling of *deja vu* experienced by Harley's long-suffering customers was further underlined when the factory followed previous custom and practice by hastily sending out a revised valvegear kit for the E, to be fitted to all 1900-odd machines produced during 1936.

Upon completion of the restitution programme, the factory asked their works rider Joe Petrali to make an attempt on the Daytona Beach mile record with a modified and lightened 61E, in an effort to reassure any remaining doubters. Petrali duly obliged, setting a new record of 136.18mph, and in the process stamping the E as the performance model in Harley's range. The E was a significant trend-setter for H-D in another way; it was the first Harley-

Previous page: Babe Tancrede, veteran Rhode Island Harley campaigner, takes another victory, this time in the Laconia 100 Mile Road Race in June 1947.

Left and right: This superbly restored 1942 model WLA 45 is one of a select group of motorcycles considered worthy of exhibit in Britain's National Motor Museum at Beaulieu, a reflection of the esteem accorded it by a war-torn generation.

Below: Harley's attack on the World Land Speed record in March 1936 was meant to have been launched by Joe Petrali on this streamlined knucklehead, but in fact his record-breaking speed of 136.18mph was set without this bodywork, as it was found to upset the handling.

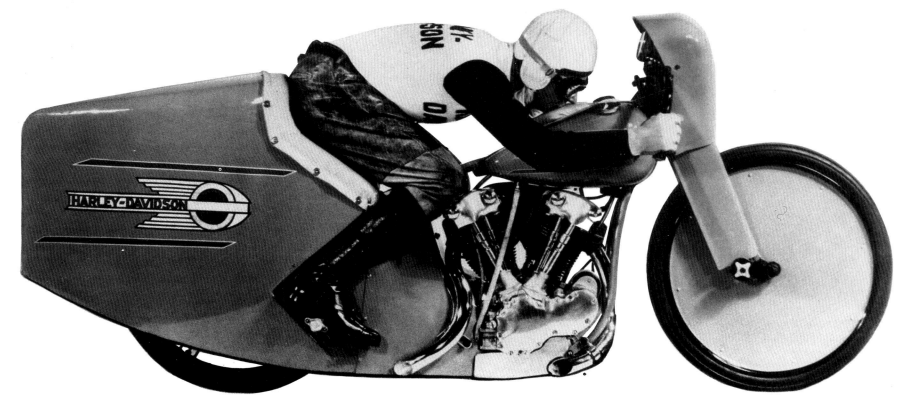

Davidson to feature a large and easily-read speedometer on a console between the two halves of the fuel tank. This styling touch has been retained on F series Harleys to this day.

More importantly, the 61E had at last put Harley-Davidson one step ahead of their long-time rivals, Indian. There was no equivalent 1000cc machine in the 'Iron Redskin' range. Their 1200 Chief was actually cheaper, but then so was Harley's own identically priced 74. The ohv 61 was in its own exclusive niche, a sports machine embodying what was, for Harley at least, modern engine technology. In late 1940, a bored and stroked 74 cubic inch version of the E was launched to run alongside the existing 61ci model. This, the first F series Harley-Davidson, showed itself to be considerably more powerful than the seminal 61, with a top speed in the region of 100mph; the extra performance was only obtained at the cost of exacerbated vibration, but with careful running-in and a reasonably realistic attitude, most enthusiasts were agreed that the gains were greater than the losses.

Three years beforehand, with depression-hit sales still languishing at around 10,000 units annually, H-D had been very much concerned with consolidation rather than experimentation. Trading on their humble origins, the founders announced two more sidevalve twins for the '37 season. The 74ci UL and its 80ci brother, the ULH, were unashamedly aimed at the conservative end of the market, being rather heavy and plodding in the old Harley tradition. With the future so uncertain, the company's cautious approach was both rational and excusable. The UL line ran successfully until 1941, proving especially popular for sidecar and police work, and fulfilling an essential function in helping to drag H-D out of the thirties depression.

The trusty old 45 was still battling on too, improved for 1937 with enhanced lubrication, cooling, and styling. In truth, it was still outshone by Indian's dynamically superior Scout, but the D's supporters came to value its solid dependability, a virtue of arguably greater importance in those straitened times. For those who wished to compete in 750cc Class C races, H-D offered the DLDR, a somewhat ersatz machine which did not really answer the enthusiasts' demands for a hotted-up thoroughbred worthy of doing dirt-track battle with the Indian Scout. Not until the arrival of the heavily-tuned WLR in 1941 would these demands be met.

Back in 1937, however, there was an unexpected crisis with the death in April of William Davidson. This was a big loss to both workforce and management. In his role of Production Head, Davidson had assumed a larger-than-life reputation on the shop floor. He had earned the respect of the ordinary men on the line, who saw him as 'one of them.' Like them, he enjoyed the simple pleasures of life, and also like them, he did not stint in the indulgence of his trencherman's appetites.

His death was coincident with a growing movement towards unionisation in the American automobile industry, a process to which 'Big Bill' was bitterly opposed. When the union's spotlight was finally turned upon the Juneau Avenue factory, Davidson's bull-headed decision to fight against the inevitable was a policy doomed to failure. Davidson's successor, William Ottaway, quickly recognised the futility of confronting the powerful United Auto Workers union, and agreed to the principle of negotiating with the union's representatives on the question of wages and conditions.

By the late 1930s, American motorcycling at the top end had taken on all the trappings of a lifestyle pastime, exemplified by the increasing profusion of clubs which went in for regular meetings, runs, social events, and bike shows. At this time, Harley-Davidson had a strong vested interest in the

Above: Easily the most famous H-D rider in the early 1940s was *Gone With The Wind* star Clark Gable. He reputedly rehearsed his lines on the bike.

Left: Excellent machine though it was, the 61-E faced stiff competition from England in the shape of bikes like this 1939 Triumph Speed Twin.

Right: WLA-derived 'rat bikes' run for ever and never lose their value.

Left: Harley-Davidson fought hard to secure and retain police contracts, pitching prices very low to squeeze the competition.

Right: The founders examine their new baby for 1947, the 125cc Hummer two-stroke, an unashamed copy (like BSA's Bantam) of the German DKW.

Below right: Another proud patrolman, this time on a Servicar trike. These models were popularly used on parking violation duties.

American Motorcycle Association, contributing most of the funds necessary for the organisation's continued existence. Through the AMA, H-D had noted the propensity of bike club members to embellish their machines with all manner of accessories. The era of the 'dresser' motorcycle had arrived. Clubs were encouraged to become affiliated to the AMA, and awards were sponsored by H-D for the 'Best Equipped' bikes at shows. The money-spinning potential of a factory-supplied accessory market was not lost on H-D's management; winning machines at club shows tended to be selected on the basis of quantity of items fitted rather than quality, owners being especially profligate in the attachment of chrome-plated running lights front and rear. This aftermarket aspect of Harley's business was a not insignificant factor in the company's road back to profitability during the late thirties and early forties.

America's national economic position in general was looking brighter by the start of the 1940s, but motorcycling was still very much a minority interest. There was a war going on in Europe, but far from plunging the States back into depression, the conflict helped to fuel the economic upturn by bringing big orders to American firms. Soon after the start of the war, both Harley-Davidson and Indian were asked to supply 5000 motorcycles by the British government following the destruction by the German air force of Triumph's factory near Coventry.

Harley's offering was the WLA, a kitted-out variant of the low-compression 45 which by then had been in production for ten years. Designed to withstand abuse, the WLA featured protective bash-plates underneath the engine and chain, high-clearance mudguards, bigger engine-cooling fins and a heavy duty air cleaner. Leather panniers, ammunition boxes and a rifle holster on the front forks completed a well-adapted package which proved itself to be perfectly suited to the rigorous demands of a wartime application.

A less effective warbike bearing the Harley-Davidson name came about as a result of the US Government's request in 1942 for H-D to produce shaft-drive flat twin military bikes along the lines of the BMW boxers which were then in widespread use by the German forces in Europe and Africa. Complying with the request, H-D came up with the sidevalve 750cc XA, only to find — not for the first time — that their new engine suffered from top-end lubrication problems. Before these almost customary faults could be rectified, a shift in the war's emphasis put a premature end to the production run after just 1000 XA's had been built. In total, Harley-Davidson produced some 88,000 motorcycles during the war, the vast majority of them WLAs, WLBs and WLCs (the Canadian version), supplemented by a smattering of 74s and 61s for police and shore patrol duties on the home front.

In the middle of the war, and within the space of less than two years, two more of the company's founders had died. President Walter Davidson's death in February 1942, at the age of 65, was from liver problems complicated by overwork. His position at the head of the boardroom table was taken by 'Big Bill's' son, William H Davidson, a long-term employee of broad experience within the managerial structure of the firm and, thanks to his late father's foresight, the biggest company shareholder also.

Then, in September 1943, William S Harley suffered a fatal heart attack at the age of 62. Harley, who was as happy photographing birds as he was designing and riding Harley-Davidsons, was succeeded as Chief Engineer by Bill Ottaway; Harley's son, William J, moved into the vice president/engineering berth. Ottaway took up his new post just in time to witness the downward turn of H-D's sales graph from its war-inspired peak years of 1942 and 1943. As the focus of the war moved to the Pacific in 1944-45 in answer to the Japanese threat, the American government cancelled its orders for military motorcycles. These machines, including some 15,000 Harley WLA's, found their way back onto both home and export markets in 1945, but they could only be sold at a government-stipulated price of $450 each.

Although H-D's wartime production figures were impressive enough, earning them fulsome commendations from the government after the war, their profit margins were so small during this period that the company was hardly any better off in financial terms than it had been before the war. One positive benefit brought about by the war was the creation in the States of a buoyant market for motorcycling among the vast numbers of soldiers returning from combat, many of whom had already experienced first-hand the Harley 45's excellent qualities of reliability and sturdiness under duress.

Unfortunately for Harley-Davidson, although the aftermath of war and the dismantling of the military machine may have paved the way for a new era of prosperity in America, the effects elsewhere effectively prevented H-D from taking advantage of the newly favorable trading conditions. The Allies had won the war — but at what price? A massively expensive regime of rationing and rebuilding had had to be implemented across most of Europe; as this came hard on the heels of the war itself, the concept of buying pricey American motorcycles was the last thing most Europeans had in mind.

Worse still for Harley-Davidson was their own government's Marshall Plan, a huge foreign aid program aimed at helping to rehabilitate Europe. The success of this plan depended on (among other things) the diversion to overseas destinations of almost all the base products produced in the US for transportation engineering-type projects. American firms attempting to regenerate their own positions at home found themselves hamstrung by severe Government restrictions on the allocation of essential materials, and hence unable to supply a market that was suddenly baying for consumer goods after a long period of enforced austerity. Adding insult to injury was the decision to relax import tariffs relating to goods brought into the States from abroad — another move designed to help in the revival of European manufacturing industries.

One such industry whose boom time had been rudely interrupted by the war was that of British motorcycling. Firms which seized the American opportunity with both hands at this time included Triumph, BSA, Norton, and Ariel, aided it must be said by the willingness of many Harley-Davidson dealers to transfer their allegiance to marques which could keep them supplied with saleable stock. Long-standing edicts handed down from Milwaukee to the dealer network, warning of the dire retribution which would befall anyone daring to sell non-Harleys alongside the home-grown product, were peremptorily pushed into the background as dealers sought to maintain their own livelihoods.

Other, more circumspect, members of the trade opted for a more 'softly softly' approach, latching on instead to the new and growing trend in cheap lightweight motorcycling, reasoning that they could get away with selling scooters from such companies as Cushman alongside the traditional heavyweight V-twins on the grounds that there was no conflict of interest. H-D appeared to accept this for a time; at least, they accepted it until the launch in 1947 of their own entry into the small two-stroke market, the 125cc Model M ('Hummer'). This machine was a straightforward copy of the DKW from Germany, the rights to produce it having been seized by the Americans and the British as part of war reparations. Britain's version was manufactured by BSA and sold under the Bantam name.

By this stage, the number of foreign motorcycles imported into the States had risen to around 15,000 units per annum, equivalent to nearly 75 percent of Harley-Davidson's total output. Most of the invaders were British middleweights of 350cc capacity, and not really ideal for riding conditions prevalent in America's most active motorcycling areas (the western states). But, by the end of the 1940s, a new breed of fast, neatly-handling 500's — including Ariel's Red Hunter and Edward Turner's classic Triumph Speed Twin — had established a much firmer following in the US. These sportsters went unchallenged by Harley-Davidson, whose smallest four-stroke was then the lumbering 45.

Those dealers who had stuck with H-D through thick and thin were understandably miffed by the factory's negative response to their suggestions that Harley should re-enter the middleweight field with something a little more adventurous than the C and a little more powerful than the similarly defunct A and B 350cc Peashooters. The company line was to point to the excellence of the 45, 61 and 74 cubic inch machines, to remind dealers of the exorbitant costs involved in designing and producing new models, and to exhort them always to emphasise the inherent superiority of 'American motorcycling' in their dealings with customers.

Above: Specialised use for the Servicar, this time as a verge-sprayer in a leafy Californian suburb.

Left: A beautiful custom panhead, capturing the '30s look in the '80s.

Right: Purists generally agree that the panhead is the most aesthetically pleasing Harley engine – with or without chrome.

Above: No big-name movie star did more to glamourise the Harley image in the 1960s than Peter Fonda. *Easy Rider* (1969) remains one of the seminal biker films.

Above right: Fonda again, this time defying authority in Roger Corman's less well known work *The Wild Angels* (1966).

Left: Another panhead special, echoing the fishtail exhaust look popularised in Fonda's films.

This latter duty was made more difficult for Harley dealers immediately after the 4 July celebrations of 1947, when a large group of Harley-riding revellers descended on the Californian town of Hollister. Although the misdemeanors which took place there over the course of a weekend were almost exclusively of a rather petty drink-related nature, *Time-Life* magazine considered it deserving of several pages provocatively illustrated by such classic photographs as the now-infamous (and reputedly 'posed') cover shot of an overweight clubman brandishing a beer bottle from the saddle of his parked Harley.

Almost overnight, motorcycling's image in the eyes of the non-riding public took a nosedive, and much of the AMA's assiduous PR work was undone at a stroke. The concept of bikers as a uniformly evil bunch of no-good hoodlums was nailed to the mast again in 1954 with the release of Stanley Kramer's feature film *The Wild One*, a Hollister-inspired fantasy starring Marlon Brando and Lee Marvin. In private life Brando actually rode a Harley, but in his film role of 'misunderstood but basically sound' rebel, he was cast as a Triumph rider. The real baddies, captained by hard-drinking Marvin, naturally rode H-Ds.

Back in the real world, 1947 was a big year for Harley-Davidson. For one, it saw the last knucklehead motors coming off the production line. The dry-sumped knucklehead engine had never managed to shake off its reputation as an oil-burner. Valve clearances had to be regularly checked and reset in the interests of engine longevity, and the choice of iron as the material for both the cylinder heads and the barrels meant that the motor was unnecessarily heavy and at the same time prone to overheating under arduous riding conditions.

The arrival in 1949 of the 'panhead' replacement motor was meant to tackle and solve all of the knucklehead's shortcomings. The barrels were still made out of iron, but the heads were now aluminum alloy for cooler and lighter running. All the engine's previously external oil lines were re-sited inside the cases, and the lubrication system was redesigned with an uprated oil pump so that crankcase pressure was no longer the less-than-dependable method employed to recirculate oil back into the holding tank.

Valves were activated by hollow, oil-filled tubes rather than the previously 'solid' valve lifters, the idea being that valve clearances would thereby be automatically maintained. Still more precise valve actuation would come about in 1953, following a decision (held by some enthusiasts to be long overdue) to reposition the lifters between the pushrods and the cam lobes, instead of in their less efficient position atop the lifter tubes, between the rocker arms and the pushrods.

From the start of its seventeen-year run, the panhead's valvegear was hidden by the chromed covers which gave the motor its nickname. Affixed to the underside of each 'pan' were felt pads, the purpose of which was to collect flying droplets of oil and then drip them back onto the valvegear as a backup to the main pump system. The pads performed the additional function of damping down the racket produced by the rocker arms. Owners were occasionally fooled by this vaguely Rube Goldberg-ish feature, thinking the pads to be some form of factory packing left inside the covers by mistake. Those home mechanics who left the pads out on re-assembly quickly learned the error of this assumption, as the increase in noise was very marked.

It almost goes without saying that there were teething troubles with the new engine, again in the lubrication department. The hydraulic valve lifters were very sensitive to changes in oil pressure, sometimes sticking at either extreme of travel. One positive (if slightly back-handed) bonus of the

TRIUMPH ENGINEERING CO. LTD., MERIDEN WORKS, ALLESLEY, COVENTRY.

Left: This 1950 ad for Triumph's potent 650cc Thunderbird development of the already popular Speed Twin only served to make life more difficult for the already beleaguered US Harley dealers. The British bike was ahead of its time; the Duo-Glide of 1958 (*below left*), by contrast, was the first Harley with suspension front and rear.

Above right: Harley's answer to the Triumph was the KH of 1952, but the answer only became effective in 1957 when it was replaced by the ohv Sportster.

Below right: Norton took their Manx 500cc singles to Daytona in the early 1950s and shocked the establishment by winning.

hydraulic system was that it reduced the likelihood of major engine damage caused by insufficient oil; without oil, the lifters simply wouldn't function, and the engine wouldn't run.

The panhead's arrival on the roads of America in 1949 was upstaged by Harley-Davidson themselves in that same year, with their long-awaited adoption of tele-hydraulic front forks. This was indeed a major change for a company which had been using springer forks since the First World War. Once more, the release of a new Harley again proved to be a searching test of their customers' patience, the teaser this time being the fitment of vented forks which occasionally sprayed their owners with oil. This quirk was ironed out before too much damage had been done, and the new model was officially christened 'Hydra-Glide' – another first, in that all previous models up to that time had gone under a simple letter designation. None of the 'handles' in popular use up until then – Knucklehead, Seventy-four, Forty-five etc – had originated from, or even been sanctioned by, the factory.

It is worth noting here that the rear end of the Hydra-Glide remained 'solid,' that is, suspended by nothing other than the bike's oversized balloon tires. Not until 1958, and the advent of the Duo-Glide, would full suspension be specified front and rear on the big FL cruisers. The rentention of a hand gearshift and foot-operated clutch was another indicator of the Hydra-Glide's underlying traditionalism.

Although Harley were more or less forced into a conservative model policy by the prevailing economic circumstances, it was a fact that by 1950 those same economic circumstances (favorable import tariffs, unfavorable export barriers) had led to a home market which was in danger of being dominated by foreign – and primarily English – manufacturers. It was also a fact that Harley-Davidson had no truly sporting motorcycles in their line-up with which to challenge the likes of Vincent's formidable 1000cc Black Shadow and Norton's Manx, a superbly-handling racer which had already begun to exert a stranglehold on the annual Daytona races.

Faced with this bleak outlook, and having only a couple of years before purchased a massive new plant on Capitol Drive in Wauwatosa, Wisconsin, in anticipation of an increase in sales which was suddenly looking less and less likely, Harley-Davidson took the unusual step of petitioning the US Government's Tariff Commission in 1951, requesting that a 40 percent import tax be imposed on all non-American motorcycles coming into the country. The petition was fiercely contested by the well-organised British Motorcycle Dealers Association, and ultimately sunk by testimony from Alfred Rich Child, one of the many disaffected ex-Harley dealers who had been on the receiving end of bullying treatment from the company in the past.

Having thus been forced to recognise that the only way to beat the Limeys was to compete with them on their own terms, Harley-Davidson entered into a new phase. The last surviving member of the original four founders, Arthur Davidson, had been killed on the day before New Year's Eve, 1950, the victim (with his wife) of an accident involving a speeding car. Although it would be untrue to say that the last traces of conservatism died with Davidson, it is certainly true that the early 1950s were busy years for H-D.

To start with, the old flathead 74 production line was finally closed down in 1952, after a four-year winding down period during which it was available only on special order by impecunious police forces outside America. At the same time, the 23-year history of the D model (the 45) was brought to a halt. Foot-operated gearshifts and conventional hand clutches were now included in the catalog, although only as an option to the foot clutch and tank-mounted gearlevers which were still standard equipment.

A new 750cc (45ci) middleweight was unveiled in the same year, featuring the foot change and hand clutch as standard. But that wasn't all. There was also suspension front and rear, and unit construction (engine and transmission in one housing) in the style of the successful British bikes. Lest Harley observers should faint at the sight of all this new technology, the new bike's flathead engine was reassuring evidence that the boys at Milwaukee had not gone completely mad.

This new middleweight, Harley's definitive answer to the foreign invaders, was assigned the letter K. It was accompanied in the catalog by a racing version, the KR, which was to take over from the flagging WR. Styling was clean and contemporary; everything looked right, in fact.

But then, the new wonderbikes went on sale.

Right: The racing KR series ran alongside the Ks, even when they were still sidevalvers like these '55 examples. The advent of the ohv versions helped to turn H-D's racing fortunes around.

Below: Another shot of the early KR sidevalve racer, complete with fender pad to allow the rider to adopt a wind-cheating posture.

New Models and Economic Problems

That Harley-Davidson should so regularly have been able to release such pal-pably imperfect new models as the K for public consumption, while still somehow managing to retain such a loyal hard core following, is a topic which almost merits a separate volume of its own. If nothing else, it is cer-tainly eloquent testimony to the marque's magnetic appeal.

As has already been mentioned, the 1952 K looked right. It undoubtedly represented a quantum leap forward from the uninspiring twenties styling of the D it was meant to replace. The powerplant was a letdown, however. Although its unit construction gave it a modern facade, the mundane side-valve format marked it down as very much the son of its father. Norton, along with a whole host of equally successful road and race machines from Italy, had proved the inherently superior power-producing capabilities of the over-head valve arrangement. Harley-Davidson themselves had sixteen years of ohv experience with the 61 and 74 big twins, but for the 45ci K they still elected to go down what was evidently expected to be an even safer flathead route.

It should have been a safer path. Extraordinary though it may seem, despite all the lessons learned in the past, the Harley engineers still had not cottoned on to the importance of proper product development. The KR racing version fell victim to early problems in the clutch department, notwith-standing the fact that its engine was actually no more powerful than its established predecessor, the WR. The straight K was revealed to be dis-appointingly sluggish, hard pressed to hit a top speed of 80mph. With a posted output of no more than 30bhp, it was patently lacking in the kind of lugging power demanded by those touring riders who preferred to travel two-up with luggage.

The K also suffered from its share of mechanical niggles, most notably a tendency to break gear teeth. Tuning parts were available to hoist the per-formance up to a more satisfactory level, and there were a few KK models produced in 1953, created by the insertion of the KR's hotter cams, polished ports and ball bearing crank into the K streetbike. By all accounts, these KKs were everything that the ordinary Ks should have been.

1953, Harley's 'Golden Anniversary' year, was celebrated with a bang: K panniers could now be ordered in the wonder material of white plastic, as well as in the usual fringed leather. In spite of this and many other anni-versary temptations, the Ks continued to languish on showroom floors, kept company only by a larger version of the DKW-derived 125cc Hummer two-stroke. This, the new Teleglide, displaced 165cc, and sat in a chassis featur-ing rudimentary telescopic forks. The new machine rekindled a smoldering interest in the small strokers, and led to the reintroduction of the 125 in 1955. Both machines then ran alongside one another in the range up to and including 1959.

The lightweight end of H-D's range might have looked reasonably healthy, but by 1954, it was painfully obvious to all – including Harley's management – that the 750cc K was desperately in need of more power. This was achieved by the commonly-used Harley expedient of lengthening the stroke by three-quarters of an inch, to give a new displacement of 54ci (883cc). The new model, designated KH, also benefitted from revisions to the clutch and transmission, and breathed more easily through larger valves. Again, there was a street/racer hybrid, the KHK, and again, this was considered to be *the* K model to buy, if only because the 'racing' innards endowed it with perform-ance to trade punches with quite ordinary imported sports machines.

Previous page: Fred Mork gives his Aermacchi-Harley single a run out at Daytona in 1985. These machines were still competing successfully at big events like the Isle of Man TT races right through until the mid 1980s.

Below left: The advent of the factory 'dresser' in the mid 60s, in the shape of the Electra Glide, legitimised a rebellious splinter group of the 50s.

Right: It didn't take long for the customisers to start work on the Duo-Glide.

Below: By the 1980s, diehards were harking back to the image, if not the lifestyle, of the 50s rebels.

Left: Another KR750 racer, this time the short-circuit version. It was also available in long track, short track, TT oval and off-road formats, a truly versatile (and eventually quite competitive) clubman racer.

Below: The Chevrolet Stingray of motorcycling in the '60s, Harley's ohv Sportster featured unit construction, light weight, short-range touring ability – and lots of image.

Let down by the factory's timidity in the choice of engine format, the K series was by no means an unqualified success for Harley-Davidson. In their defense, H-D did experiment in the mid fifties with an all-aluminum engined replacement for the K, the KL, and even got as far as testing a running prototype before guillotining the project. This error was to be put right in 1957, one year after the KH's discontinuation, with the resounding arrival of the XL Sportster.

Before that happened, however, in 1955 the 74ci Panhead's bottom end was beefed up with sturdier main bearings, leaving the motor wide-open for the ex-works horsepower enhancement. To reflect this new 'high perform-ance' aspect, the designation for the F was changed to FLH, a letter-code which is still used today to denote definitive big twin Harleys.

The spark of excitement thus lit among H-D disciples grew to fever pitch two years later, with the 1957 launch of the XL Sportster. In reality, it was nothing more than a logical development of the KH. Practically identical to it in most respects, it differed only in one major aspect: the provision of a decently powerful overhead valve engine. Although there were few visible differences between the old and the new engines, the Sportster reflected rather more advanced thinking in regard to the extraction of a more refined kind of power. Reverting to the original 750cc K's shorter stroke, the XL achieved the KH's extra displacement of 883cc by an increase in the bore. This approach, now widely accepted in modern tuning applications, allowed a higher rev ceiling by virtue of a decrease in piston speed, which in turn had been made possible by the shortening of the stroke. While low-down torque was compromised by this tuning method, the bonus came in the form of en-hanced smoothness at high rpm. Bigger pistons also allowed for bigger valves on the Sportster, improving engine breathing. The overall result was 40 horsepower at 5500rpm, figures which on a Harley-Davidson sales bro-chure must have seemed quite staggering.

Complaints concerning the inaccessibility of the old Ks transmission com-ponents led H-D's engineers to fit a 'trapdoor' in the Sportster's gearcase. The gears themselves were shifted by a lever under the rider's right foot, a

Above left: The ingenuity of the custom Harley builder knows no bounds. This fully street legal double-engined shovelhead was spotted at Daytona.

Above: The engine has always been the focal point of any custom Harley. This 74 features exquisite engraving.

Left: The racing version of the ohv Sportster went under the XLR model name. With 82bhp from its 883cc, it won races both on its native dirt tracks and on some European road circuits.

nod in the direction of the British bikes that were still prevalent in sporting circles at that time. Although the new machine's image was overtly sporting, the factory endeavored to spread the Sportster's appeal by offering such factory options as panniers, screens and luggage racks. By this unsubtle device, Harley-Davidson hoped to cast the Sportster as a multi-purpose machine which might possibly be perceived as a smaller version of the FLH tourer.

In the event, this role-modelling fooled no one. It was plain that the Sportster had at last tapped into the potentially rich sportbike seam which had theretofore eluded Harley-Davidson. At long last, here was a home-grown, 100mph American motorcycle capable of overpowering the upstart Triumphs – in a straight line, anyway. Soggy coil suspension at the rear and inaccurate steering at high speed tended to confine Sportster riders' exuberance around corners. The package was nonetheless an instant hit.

For the 58 season, power was lifted still further for the new XLH model, by raising the compression ratio from an innocuous 7.5:1 to a rather more purposeful 9:1, and by the fitment of still larger valves. But America's excited motorcycling enthusiasts wanted even more; the XLCH was Harley's answer. Magneto ignition, high-level separate exhaust pipes and a small 'peanut' fuel tank distinguished the 'Competition Hot' XL from its humbler cousins. Strangely, the 1959 XLCH came with semi-knobbly off-road type tires, even though its true milieu was plainly the street. Factory publicity shots of the time show gritted-teeth company representatives hurling XLCH's up and down hills, presumably in an effort to persuade buyers that the Sportster's potential market extended all the way out to dirt riders. Needless to say, few buyers of what was after all still a heavyweight machine (nearly 500 pounds) cared to take up the off-road option.

By 1959, all XL derivatives had been given higher performance camshafts, hiking horsepower up to a claimed 55bhp. This period in American motorcycling history was marked by a general demand for more and more horsepower, to be used not only on the streets but also on the quarter-mile drag strips that were becoming increasingly popular towards the end of the 1950s. Harleys were especially handy for this latter purpose, being eminently susceptible to both weight-trimming and tuning. 'Hot' engine parts were readily available from any one of a myriad of aftermarket outlets which had been set up specifically to attend to the needs of those heretics who insisted on modifying their H-Ds. Harley-Davidson frowned upon this practice,

Left: A '70s shovelhead motor inside an aftermarket hardtail frame – a popular expression of individuality among Harley riders which is now being tapped by the factory.

Right: The archetypal 'crucifix' look: not as uncomfortable as it looks.

Below: Standard factory aircleaners might be legal, but they strangle performance. Big power gains are available by swapping carbs too.

as did their more dyed-in-the-wool dealers, with the unbelievable result that many of them would refuse to service or tune machines which had been so altered.

A widening division thus began to open up between the 'respectable' dresser-riding Harley owners and the shadier, denim-wearing 'outlaw' elements who, although just as organised and non-individualistic in their own way, still liked to think they were thumbing their noses at authority. Whether they realised it or not, Harley-Davidson were contributing to this rift by producing two such divergent machines as the Sportster and the FLH supercruiser. Perversely, the outlaw riders tended to favour FLs as base vehicles for their customising efforts, an attitude which only served to enrage the traditionalists all the more.

As 1960 came around, non-traditionalists were still bemoaning the lack of a true middleweight in the Harley range. H-D themselves were concerned by the fact that their annual production figures had been more or less constant throughout the previous decade, hovering around 12-15,000 units in the second half of the fifties, after having started off the decade with annual sales closer to 20,000. A chance to kill two birds with one stone came up in 1960, when H-D's management heard the news that Aermacchi, a successful but underfunded Italian sports motorcycle manufacturer in Varese, were casting around for partners to help them break into new markets. After a short period of negotiation, Harley were able to purchase a 50 percent share in Aermacchi at a bargain price, setting up a situation whereby the Italians' best machine, the 250cc Ala Verde four-stroke single, could be imported into the States under the H-D banner.

Sadly, Harley's timing was wrong. The 'Sprint', as it was entitled for Stateside consumption, was introduced onto the American market just as the superior (and cheaper) four-stroke singles and twins from Japan were starting to arrive. Compounding the problem was the lingering antipathy displayed toward the 'Italian Harleys' by the less progressive dealers in the US network. In fairness, many of the dealers' misgivings were justified, in that many Americans thought it demeaning to be seen riding a foreign bike. Even worse, the Aermacchi was not just a foreign bike; it was a *small* foreign bike. The combination was doomed to failure.

And if that lot wasn't enough, there were inevitably problems associated with the sheer distance between Milwaukee and Varese. Although H-D always had representatives on site in Italy, these men were quickly frustrated by the discovery that American 'get tough' techniques were not re-

cognised by imperturbable Latin types in times of difficulty. The Sprint (supplemented from 1962 by the off-road H, or Sprint Scrambler) did as well as could be expected under these impossibly adverse conditions, its sales record being more notable for its length (thirteen years) than for its volume.

The Italians were nothing if not prolific, however, as evidenced by the throwing-up of a 50cc two-stroke minibike between 1966 and 1968, namely the Leggero M-50. This machine grew to 65cc in '68, from which point it ran parallel with the 125cc Rapido, an uninspiring little 10bhp runabout which stuck around until the end of the 1970s. From '73 to '77 these bikes were joined in a somewhat confusing line-up by the SS range of two-stroke singles, in 125, 175, and 250cc sizes, and by a new 350 Sprint four-stroke single.

Although all these motorcycles bore the name of Harley-Davidson on their tanks, the gulf between them and the 'real' H-Ds was so great that nobody who bought one of the Italian lightweights seriously considered himself (or herself) to be a true Harley owner. The two-strokes were soon consigned to the rubbish heap of history anyway, victims of the anti-pollution paranoia that was sweeping across the States in the mid-seventies — yet another example of unfortunate timing by Harley-Davidson. The Varese link was finally severed in June 1978 with the closure of the factory in Italy. The facility was later bought by Cagiva, who went on to build many thousands more of lightweight SS/SX type two-strokes (primarily for the European market) before expanding into a motorcycling monolith in the mid-1980s with the capture of the classic Italian marque, Ducati.

Back in 1960, Harley-Davidson were again displaying their occasional tendency to produce the wrong thing at the wrong time. This time they were attempting to enter the scooter market. Their Topper offering was a heavy-bodied affair — what else from H-D? — powered by what turned out to be a too-lightweight engine, the Teleglide's 165cc two-stroke unit. Too small for the highway, too cumbersome for urban work, the 5bhp belt-driven hybrid limped on until 1965, when it was 'souped up' to 9bhp in a last attempt to inject it with some sales-generating pep. The damage had been done by then, sadly; the Topper was axed in that same year.

Paradoxically, while mistakes were undoubtedly being made during this late fifties-early sixties period of exploration of uncharted territories, racing

Above: For many, the Electra Glide represents the rolling embodiment of American excess.

Above right: Stripped of its bodywork and luggage boxes, the Electra Glide takes on an entirely different 'retro' identity. Again, the factory have latched onto this nostalgia-driven trend, and are nowadays producing their own 'stripped' Glides.

Right: The ultimate double-take?

Right: When the Electra Glide became the Tour Glide, handling improved along with everything else. For its size, the FLT is surprisingly easy to ride at the limit.

Left and below: Weight was never a major consideration for riders into serious personalisation of their Electra Glides.

Harleys were enjoying some of their best years on the native oval tracks that were so well suited to their particular brand of raw wheel-sliding power. The KRs and KHRs that had started out so unimpressively eventually metamorphosed into highly adaptable and winning machines, campaigned with great verve and localised success right up until the late sixties.

In 1963, Harley-Davidson bought the Tomahawk Boat Company, a fiberglass plant in northern Wisconsin which was originally intended to slot into the H-D jigsaw as a supplier of bodies for Servi-cars, sidecars and golf carts. From 1969, fairings, pannier cases and other fiberglass sundries were also sourced from Tomahawk.

1964 saw the fitment of a full-width brake drum to the Sportster's front wheel. Otherwise things were beginning to stagnate. By 1965, Harley's position was suddenly perceived to be far from stable. Precious little development had taken place in the big twin range. The company had been marking time, selling only a few thousand FLs every year, and even fewer XLs. Total annual production was struggling to top four figures, Aermacchis included, despite the fact that the company owned massive — albeit outmoded — production facilities. According to the figures, the company's turnover had increased substantially since the late fifties, but nowhere near as substantially as it should have done. Profit margins were unbelievably small, and the model range dormant; neither was there any immediate prospect of the situation changing, since there was no cash available for much-needed investment in the machine tooling necessary for new model development. Money had to be raised — and quickly.

The decision to 'go public' precipitated a series of share offers during the course of 1965 and 1966. While such an offer nowadays would result in a stampede of investors beating a path to Milwaukee, it was apparently not such an attractive proposition in 1965. The number of shareholders was small, in the hundreds rather than the thousands, and a big enough proportion of them were sufficiently closely connected to the Harley and Davidson families to ensure that control of the company did not fall into outside hands.

Funds duly raised, it was deemed appropriate to devote some attention to the FL cruiser. Since being given a more effective — though still somewhat inadequate — braking system in 1958 (disk brakes not becoming standard equipment until 1972), this trusty model had been rather neglected. For 1965, the electrical system was upgraded from six volts to twelve, an electric starter was grafted onto the engine behind the cylinder block — and the Electra Glide was born. In a repeat of a similar Luddite outburst many years previously when front brakes had first been fitted to the big twins, a significant number of owners and dealers protested that the electric starter was a retrograde step. With some justification, they pointed out that it was easy enough to start the softly-tuned 1200cc twin engine; they also queried the extra 75 pounds which was the weight penalty of the electrical conversion.

While the electric start had long been a common fixture on Japanese motorcycles, it was quite revolutionary for the FL, a machine which after all could still be ordered with a hand gearchange (this option running on until the 1973 model year). The engineers were not unaware of the performance-sapping aspects of their modifications. They also knew that a new engine was on the stocks, scheduled to come into production the following year. As a stopgap measure, to help the panhead engine cope with its extra duties, the compression ratio was raised and the cam profiles revised for a new (claimed) power output of 60bhp, an increase of a little more than 10 percent. With the compression ratio increase, the 'easy starting' argument had, at a stroke, become slightly less tenable.

A larger five-gallon fuel tank was also added at this time, although it was still dwarfed by the Electra Glide's slightly absurd 'overgrown bicycle seat', a well stuffed perch (usually supplied in highly impractical light colors) which looked comfortable from a distance but which was in reality too big for a solo rider and too small for a pillion. Critics also noted the disappearance of the tool box, squeezed out of the chassis by the Electra Glide's enlarged battery box. Tools would not reappear on Harley-Davidsons until the 1980s, and only then as an expensive option. They were very high quality, however.

Predictably, there were warranty claims on the first all-electric FLs. The starters gave trouble, and in the wrong hands the motor's extra power could

Left: The alloy-engined XR750 dirtracker achieved extraordinary dominance on the American circuit throughout the 60s and 70s, and was still competitive in the late 80s.

Right: The shorty helmet 'patrolman' look has become associated with civilian Electra Glide motorcycling.

— and did — place a breaking stress on the relatively spindly final drive chain. New, stronger parts were sent out in the time-honored way. By this time it must have been increasingly obvious to experienced H-D customers that the best time to buy a brand new model was most assuredly not in its first year of manufacture.

There was accordingly some degree of agonising among the serried ranks of the faithful in 1966, when Milwaukee made a double announcement: the end of the Panhead after 18 years of generally good service, and the birth of its successor, the 74 cubic inch 'Shovelhead.' Like the Sportster, the Shovelhead featured rocker arms pivoting inside castings bolted to the cylinder heads. These castings were somewhat fancifully reckoned to resemble coal shovels, hence the nickname. Unlike the smaller Sportster motor, the 74 shovel retained the separate transmission format already established through long usage. In the eyes of many enthusiasts, the new motor represented the ultimate V-twin development — in theory, at least. The apparent oil-tightness of the engines in practice was further cause for celebration.

Harley-Davidson thought highly of it too, dubbing their Electra Glide 'King Of The Highway' by way of acknowledgment. If sheer physical size was the criterion, no other motorcycle manufacturer could challenge this grandiose-sounding claim, for a fully-fuelled FLH now tipped the scales at just a few pounds short of the 800 pound mark. Nonetheless, in spite of its incredible bulk, the bike remained well balanced and easy to ride at low speeds, thanks mainly to its gratifyingly low center of gravity. By contrast, behavior at speeds anywhere near the beast's 100mph maximum was unruly enough to make most riders think twice about exploring the upper reaches of performance. Suspension was too soft and ground clearance too low for any liberties to be taken. Most riders knew and accepted this, and stayed well within the FLH's limits as a consequence.

Though well received, the arrival of the new shovelheaded Electra Glides and Sportsters had not been enough to revitalise the company. By the end of 1967, it was clear to the management that more stock issues would not be enough either. the kind of major financial input required to ensure the company's future could only be obtained in one way. A 'white knight' had to be found, in the shape of a strong but benevolent corporation which would take over Harley-Davidson — preferably without disturbing the status quo.

After a protracted and complicated battle with the New York-based firm Bangor Punta, during which the value of Harley-Davidson shares multiplied several times, Rodney C Gott's giant leisure products conglomerate, AMF — the American Machine & Foundry Company — finally came through and emerged as victors.

Takeover was scheduled for January of 1969 — and a dark chapter in Harley's history was about to be opened.

Left: Jay Springsteen takes the back straight jump on an American 'TT' dirt track. Springsteen's name became all but synonymous with victory during his heyday on the XR750.

Right: Springsteen with his tuning guru Bill Werner — an unbeatable combination. The XR motor had exactly the right type of power delivery for fast and efficient loose-surface broadsliding.

The Best Harleys Ever?

The story of AMF and Harley-Davidson can be told in one sentence. In January 1969, AMF paid $21 million for Harley-Davidson; in June 1981, they sold the company for $80 million.

Set out in such bald terms, it sounds like a perfectly run of the mill example of a successful business undertaking. But behind the impressive figures lies an eleven year history of confusion, turbulence, bitterness and greed, seasoned by an almost ceaseless conflict of interest between AMF and H-D.

AMF's motives in buying Harley-Davidson were not far removed from those of H-D's founders who wanted to sell; both parties wished to realise a quick profit. But, while AMF's board of directors and those Harley share-holders whose main wish it was to make a final exit from the precarious world of motorcycle manufacture were both well satisfied by the deal, the general air of contentment soon turned sour – on both sides.

On completion of the purchase formalities in January 1969, Harley-Davidson made an announcement to the effect that there would be no visible change in the way the company went about its business, other than that there would of course now be a period of new-model-driven success, since funds had at last been made available for product development. AMF, for their part, were busy conducting a major investigation into the state of the company they had just bought. The results of this investigation were not encouraging.

Previous page: The stark black paint scheme enhances the looks of this 1979 XLCR 1000.

Above: AMF's attempts to diversify the Harley range with machines like the 125-250cc two-stroke single SX models enjoyed some sales success, but these bikes were not recognised as 'real' Harleys.

Top right: At the other end of the scale, Cal Rayborn took time out from a glittering road race career in 1970 to go for the world speed record in this factory-supported 89ci Sportster streamliner. His speed was 265.492mph.

Management appeared to be in disarray, a throwback to the days when all decisions were taken by the four original founders. Marketing seemed to be non-existent, with no realistic indication as to the direction in which the company was heading. Chances to restructure the company had been ignored; new model development had been similarly spurned; and the whole company ethos appeared to be heavily biased towards cost-cutting and the maximisation of short term profits.

This latter approach dovetailed nicely with Harley's non-interventionist policy on new models, but the feeling among AMF's upper management was that H-D had been 'getting away with it' for too long. A more dynamic position had to be established. The ohv V-twin engine that had been powering Harleys in basically unchanged format since 1936 was considered long overdue for major revamping – if not actual scrapping. Harley-Davidson's view was, not surprisingly, rather different. They were able to point to the continuing racetrack successes still being enjoyed by such riders as Cal Rayborn on KR's powered by even more primitively-conceived engines than the shovelheads that were under criticism. They also maintained that the strong heritage of conservatism running through their customer profile could easily lead to mass rejection of anything that might be seen as too 'new-fangled.'

Sweeping aside H-D's misgivings, AMF embarked upon an expensive program of re-tooling for the Juneau Avenue and Capitol Drive plants. This move, while not greatly benefiting Harley's fortunes during AMF's period of ownership, was to prove crucially important in safeguarding the company's future after AMF's departure.

In the meantime, Harley continued with their own relatively humble but ongoing development plans. Breakerless ignition was specified for the 1970 FLs, and the new 350cc four-stroke from Aermacchi was added to the line-up for that model year. A new racing motorcycle, the XR750, was designed and built to take over from the KR. This machine, powered by a downsized and tuned version of the 883cc Sportster engine, was to be made available in both flat track and fully-faired circuit racer options. Making full use of their influence over the AMA, Harley secured an agreement from the sport's governing body for the old Class C regulations to be broadened to take in overhead-valve engines. The new XRs went on from there, ushering in yet another golden age for H-D's competition department. They proved especially dominant on the half-mile, mile, and 'TT' dirt courses from the time of the factory's transition to alloy engines in 1972 right up to the model's eventual demise in 1985, at which point it was still competing successfully.

Above: Probably the best shovelhead – the Low Rider.

Left: A modern classic H-D – the Super Glide 1200, pictured at Daytona's Boot Hill Saloon.

Below: A 1976 Sportster from the ill-fated AMF era.

Above: Now rapidly becoming collectable (though not necessarily in this rather lurid non-standard paintjob), the XLCR1000 Cafe Racer looked like it went – mean and moody.

Left: The Super Glide of 1979, complete with convoluted factory exhaust headers.

Near right: H-D chairman Vaughn Beals (seated) celebrates the listing of his company on the New York Stock Exchange in 1986.

Far right: Flying the flags at Harley's factory, one of the last bastions of US patriotism.

Although it may not have seemed so at the time, the launch in 1970 of the FX 'Super Glide' can now be viewed as one of the most momentous events in Harley-Davidson's history. The 74 cubic inch (1200cc) 'Glide', a simple amalgam of the XL Sportster's front end and the FL frame/engine package, was offered in kick-start (FX) and electric start (FXE) options. Its singular plainness, as evidenced by the total lack of Electra Glide-type bodywork, was the very feature which made it so unusual. It represented the factory's first recognition of the fact that there were other kinds of H-D rider other than the straight-backed mature clubmen whom it had up to then fondly imagined to be its exclusive clientele.

Brainchild of the design department's Willie G Davidson (son of Chief Executive William H Davidson, and unquestionably the highest-profile 'biker' on the board), the FX was a perfect base machine for customising. This practice, previously regarded with a kind of sniffy hauteur by H-D, had been so facilitated by the explosion of aftermarket parts outlets, and so glamorised by motion pictures such as Easy Rider, that it had become virtually impossible to ignore. On the somewhat grudging basis of 'if you can't beat 'em, join 'em,' H-D had finally locked into the populist groove which was destined to steer them through the murky waters ahead. Later on, in the 1980s, the company's conversion in this direction was completed by their wholehearted entry into the immensely profitable arena of 'factory approved' custom parts and accessories.

Back in 1970, meanwhile, a new corporate logo had been created. It featured a prominent figure '1' and referred to Harley-Davidsons as 'The All-American Freedom Machines,' but problems on the production line in AMF's first few months of command turned this proud boast into a sick joke for a large number of dealers and customers. An integral part of AMF's crusade to wrench H-D into the twentieth century was a determination to crank the line up to automobile speed; unfortunately, this plan was at severe odds with the existing production facilities in Milwaukee. There was simply not enough time, space or technology in the Juneau Avenue works to meet the doubled targets newly set by AMF's line controllers. Quality control went out of the window as staff worked feverishly to build over 50,000 motorcycles a year. Many experienced workers had had enough and quit in disgust, further exacerbating the problems.

The atmosphere in the factory was at an all-time low. Out in the country, H-D dealers were aghast at the state of some of the machines they were receiving from the factory. And of course, as usual, they were the ones who were obliged to spend time and money making those machines saleable. In many cases, the bikes were so appallingly put together that they could not be made to work at all. In the final analysis, it took over two years to put matters to rights, by which time it had become a positive stigma to be seen running an 'AMF Harley'. Even now, bikes built in this era tend to be shunned by buyers in the secondhand market.

In 1971, in the midst of the quality scandal, AMF attempted to bring order to the situation by transferring a large part of the assembly process to one of their existing factory premises in York, Pennsylvania. Engines and transmissions continued to be built at the Capitol Drive works in Milwaukee, and then trans-shipped to York for mating with the chassis and cycle parts. Two years later, in 1973, the historic Juneau Avenue facility became a warehouse-cum-office complex. The severing of old links had been tragically underlined in August of '71 with the death of William J Harley, son of founder Bill Harley, and less traumatically by the resignation from the Vice Presidency of Walter Davidson Jr, nephew of Arthur Davidson.

1971 was a big year for the Sportster, in every sense. The XL motor was taken out to the 61ci (1000cc) size which many pundits had said it should have displaced from the start. The extra power thus created was to some extent vitiated by the commensurate increase in the amount of heat and vibration generated. It also further highlighted the shortcomings of the four-speed transmission, with its sticky action and its big jump in ratios from third to top. This latter expedient, intended to provide reasonable smoothness at the 55mph freeway speed limit, only did so at the expense of tractability in town. It was to be some years before H-D would properly address this question.

By 1973, Harley president William H Davidson decided he had had enough and retired, to be replaced by John O'Brien, one of AMF's production experts. A drive to weed out the less dynamic H-D dealers ensued, the idea being to put the company in a better position to defend itself from the rapidly growing Japanese threat. Fuelled by what turned out to be a false dawn in America's economic outlook, production was by then running at record levels, with over 70,000 motorcycles built in 1973 alone. The quality control

difficulties were still blighting the company's image, however. AMF supervisors on the shop floor were becoming increasingly frustrated by their inability to change the customs and practices of decades.

Behind their desks, the AMF directors were also becoming increasingly convinced that they had bought a pig in a poke, a dry and empty hulk which had already had all the profitability squeezed out of it by successive generations of the Harley and Davidson dynasties. Even though vast sums of money had been pumped in by AMF, there seemed to be no way of turning the company back out of the cul-de-sac into which it had been driven by H-D's over-cautious model policy. The FLs had become expensive anachronisms in a marketplace newly populated by Japanese mega-tourers of superior performance, such as Honda's Gold Wing. The Sportster was likewise being ridiculed by mold-breaking superbikes such as Kawasaki's 900cc Z1. Worse still, the Middle Eastern oil-producing nations had hoisted the price of crude to a level which was suddenly threatening the viability of all heavy industrial concerns, Harley-Davidson among them.

While considering their next move, AMF began recruiting engineers to work on H-D's listing ship. One of those engineers, Vaughn Beals, found himself lashed to the helm. By the end of 1977, his view from the bridge was daunting, to say the least. Annual production had dropped back down to 45,000 from a '76 figure of 61,000; a new Sportster variant, the XLCR Cafe Racer, had bombed in the showrooms; and there was a strong suspicion that the big four Japanese firms were 'dumping' their excess production on the American market, undercutting H-D by discounting their bikes to incredibly low price levels.

In 1978, AMF paid heavily for the luxury of testing this suspicion in front of the government's Tariff Commission. As had happened in 1951, H-D's case was effectively killed off by testimony from their own dealers, who gave vent to many years' worth of pent-up bile by denigrating Harley's regressive attitude in regard to model development and other matters. As had happened in 1951, the Commission listened closely to the damning evidence before throwing out H-D's claim of unfair Japanese competition.

Left: Late 80s Evolution-engined FXRS Low Rider is arguably the best all-round Harley street bike yet.

Right: Believe it or not, this 'hogged out' drag-racer style 93-incher started off life as a police bike.

Below right: Highest profile descendant of the founders still working for the old firm is Willie G Davidson. He has masterminded the styling changes which have revolutionised sales in recent years.

Left: 1987 Softail Custom married traditional hardtail look with the convenience of hidden suspension.

Right: Harleys are now finding their way into the garages of well-heeled professional types. . .

Below right: . . .as well as into the hearts of true enthusiasts who mortgage their houses to buy one.

Below: HOG (Harley Owners Group) liaises with factory on product policy matters.

Licking their wounds, AMF's bosses fell back in a disorderly retreat to the bread and butter business of selling – or attempting to sell – motorcycles. To rekindle some interest in the ancient FL, its engine size was increased to the old sidevalver's capacity of 80 cubic inches (around 1340cc). By 1980, all the FLs and FXs were powered by this motor, killing off the once-classic 74ci/1200cc class (the 1200 would actually return to the range in the late 1980s, but only in the Sportster's unit construction format). A much more welcome step forward was the provision of a five-speed transmission on the 1980 FLT tourer, an advance which combined with vibration-isolating engine and footboard mounts to make this the most relaxed cruiser ever to bear the H-D badge.

Further evidence of the company's new-found commitment to enhanced rider comfort was to be found on the 1980 Sturgis, a new variation on the 'stripped-look' FX theme. Named after the annual bike rally venue in the Dakota hills, the all-black Sturgis was distinguished by its toothed-belt final drive. The claim that this would provide up to 50,000 miles of lubrication-free, adjustment-free motorcycling was not always borne out, and there were additional complications attendant upon the replacement procedure, but the Kevlar-reinforced Gates belt undoubtedly made a noticeable contribution to the FX's quietness and smoothness in operation. The Sturgis and the FLT, both of which were benchmark machines in their own way, had been designed by Erik Buell. A talented engineer, Buell subsequently left H-D to set up his own business producing purposeful XR1000-based specials aimed at the 'Battle of the Twins' races, first instituted at Daytona in the mid 1980s.

1980 was the crunch year for AMF. Cutting their losses, and having failed to find a suitable outside buyer, they offered Harley-Davidson up to a management-led buyout group headed by Vaughn Beals. Following lengthy negotiations throughout 1980 and the early part of 1981, the handover was finally completed on 1 June 1981, with Beals becoming the new Chairman. Reaffirming his commitment to the principle of combining the best aspects of the old and the new, Beals set out on the long and uphill road towards re-establishment of Harley's once-great name.

The journey began, symbolically at least, with an organised ride by members of the new management from the York assembly plant (which had been given over to the buyout group by AMF as part of the deal) to the Milwaukee engine-building facility. The last echoes of the takeover hullabaloo had only just died down when the cold shadow of economic recession fell across Harley's portals – not for the first time. Inflation was eroding the saleability of H-D's products from one side, while the continued landing of massive quantities of Japanese motorcycles in American ports was chipping great lumps out of their customer base. Discounting was once again rife, but even the

truly desperate discounting measures taken by the Japanese to reduce their massive overstocking in the States proved inadequate.

H-D were hit very hard at this time. Hundreds of workers had to be laid off as domestic sales all but dried up. A new stripped-to-the-bone Sportster, the XLX-61, was released with a bargain price tag of just $3995 in an attempt to stimulate some showroom action, and streamlined new 'materials as needed' (MAN) production line techniques were brought into force. This latter move gave rise to real financial benefits in the longer term, and to increased worker contentment in the short and long terms. But the short term financial benefits were not so easily gained. The company's financial position was still parlous.

So it was that in early 1983, Harley-Davidson were obliged to petition the Tariff Commission for a third time in search of relief from the damaging effects of cheap Japanese imports. Much preparatory effort went into ensuring that their case would seem more reasoned than it had on the two previous abortive occasions. Rather than tarring all Japanese motorcycles

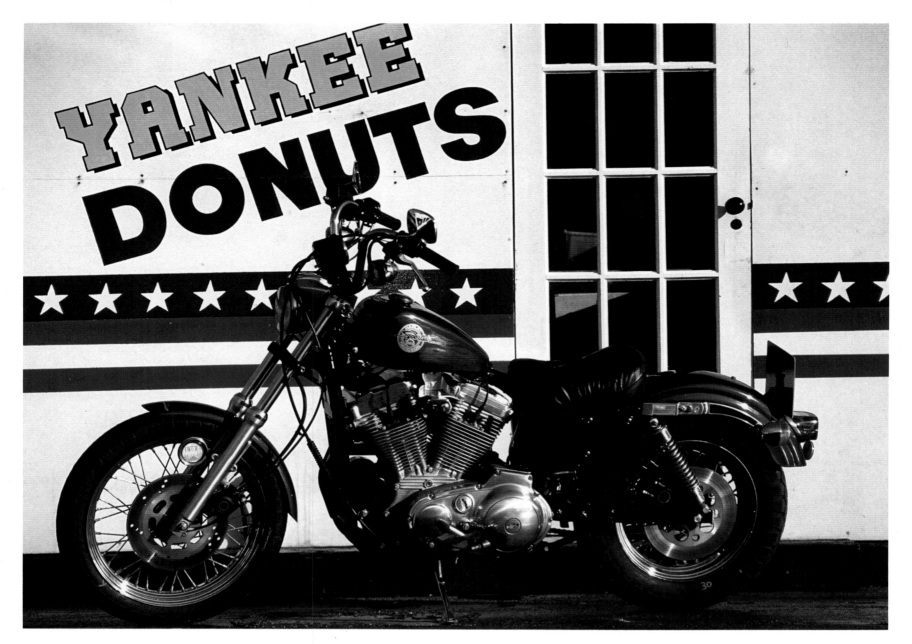

Above: Harley ownership was brought within the reach of the mass biking population in the 1980s with the arrival of the $3995 Sportster 883.

Left: For a reasonable extra outlay, the base Sportsters could be easily transformed into poky 1200s.

Right: The stuff of which dreams are made – a shiny new Sportster, fresh out of the crate.

with the same brush, H-D's representatives sought to penalise only those displacing 700cc or more, since these were the only machines which could reasonably be claimed to have had an adverse effect on Harley's own sales.

The tactic worked, and in April 1982 brought onto the statute books a sliding scale of import tariffs which would diminish from high to low over a five-year period. The idea was to give Harley-Davidson some breathing space in which to establish themselves as true competitors in the American motorcycle market. Although the Japanese government initially threatened to erect retaliatory barriers in protest at the Commission's decision, discretion eventually proved the better part of valor. In the long run, there was some political expediency in graceful acceptance of the situation – quite apart from the very real possibility of terminally alienating the American consumer as a consequence of what would have been ill-advised direct action. As it happened, Harley's situation had improved so markedly before the end of the five-year period that they were able to offer to discard the protective cloak which they had fought so hard to drape around themselves.

1983 saw the formation – by H-D – of the 'Harley Owners Group', a choice of title which incidentally recognised the 'hog' nickname that had long been part of the Harley *argot*. At this time, rumors concerning H-D's collaboration with Porsche on the design of an all-new multivalve engine were gaining currency, but the new engine that actually made it out of the R&D shop in 1983 was the V2 Evolution motor.

As in previous reincarnations of the Milwaukee V-twin, the 'Evo' was externally identifiable by its new rocker boxes. Also new this time around was the use of aluminum alloy for both heads and cylinders. The ignition system featured twin advance curves, while the motor burned unleaded fuel in spite of its higher compression ratio. Pistons were flat-topped instead of domed, and ran inside iron liners.

The new motor soon showed itself to be both powerful and, a first for Harley, just about oil-tight. It was first featured in the new FXRS Sport Glide, an unfaired FX derivative with rubberised engine mounts and unprecedentedly generous ground clearance. The combination of the new engine in this excellent chassis resulted in what was without question the best all-round stock machine ever to roll off the H-D production line. Journalists who had previously either criticised all Harleys or acted as apologists for them were relieved to find a Milwaukee machine which could at last be fairly compared, like for like, with other 'normal' motorcycles.

Better yet, there were increasingly positive signs that the quality control problem was well on the way to being conquered. Warranty claims were well down, and the deep sheen of the paintwork and chroming was redolent of earlier and better times. Improved reliability records (and a very favorable tender) even persuaded the influential Californian Highway Patrol police force to switch back to Harleys after a long spell aboard Kawasakis.

The new model for 1983 turned out to be a high performance version of the Sportster, the XR1000. What started out as a good idea somehow lost its way between the drawing board and the showroom; fast-sounding engine internals were fitted inside what was effectively the cheapest Sportster (the XLX), and a whopping price tag of a whisker under $7000 was attached to the result. Although real performance could be obtained by further expenditure on a factory-approved tuning kit, the basic machine was still a

Above left: Going into the 90s, the Sportster's classic lines are finding more support from a motorcycling public increasingly disenchanted by the offerings from Japan.

Below left: New lamps for old – the modern Heritage Softail (foreground) rubs shoulders with its knuckleheaded forebear.

Right: Oh, for a giant-size shopping trolley. . . Evolution engines await shipment.

Overleaf: The revival of the springer front end struck a chord among old and young customers, and worked reasonably well too.

Left: The only real drawback with the Softail Springer, in the wet at any rate, was the limited grip offered by its skinny front tire.

Right and below: The Heritage Softail, featuring a solidly-mounted Evolution engine, hearkened back to the hardtail Hydra Glide of the 1950s.

base model Sportster, with all the shortcomings that that entailed. XR1000 production ran for a couple of years and then faded away, a sad end to what could so easily have been a great bike.

Willie G Davidson's evident willingness to spend time with and listen to the people who were buying his motorcycles was also beginning to show dividends in the mid-1980s. Taking an ever greater role in all aspects of product design, Davidson quickly identified a nostalgic element in the aspirations of customers both old and young, potential or existing. The FX 'Softail' of 1984 was the first tentative realisation-in-the-metal of this apparent yearning.

Embodying the styling appeal of the old rigid-rear-ended classics of the forties and fifties, and the comfort and sophistication of a hidden underframe suspension system, the Softail offered the best of old and new in a single attractive package. Originally sold with a four-speed transmission and kickstart lever so as to emphasise its traditionalism, even these sops to the die-hards were abandoned after the 1985 model year in favor of five speeds and an electric foot. Additional transmission sophistication was brought to bear on the 80-inchers in mid-1984, with the incorporation of a wet multiplate clutch. The solid engine mounts remained on some models, however (including the Softail), making available the dubious pleasure of Harley's equally 'traditional' hammering vibrations to anyone who cared to explore the upper reaches of the engine's rev range.

Diversification was the name of the game in the mid 1980s, with the purchase of a three-wheel sports car manufacturer (Trihawk) in '84 and the securing of various contracts to make gunshell casings for the US Navy. While the Trihawk connection is at the time of writing still to be exploited in any obvious way, the munitions contracts have proved very lucrative, allowing H-D to move into yet more areas outside motorcycling. Their purchase of the highly profitable Holiday Rambler motorhome group in 1986 was perhaps the most visible example of these new-found acquisitional activities, although British enthusiasts will doubtless also recall Harley's takeover of the Armstrong off-road motorcycle specialists in 1988.

1986 was notable for the unveiling of the Evolution-powered Sportsters, available once more in the old 883cc capacity as well as in 1100 and (later) 1200cc alternatives. The transmission ratios were closed up a little too, but the real solution – a five-speed box – is yet to make an appearance. The ultimate expression of H-D's nostalgia-driven return to prosperity did make its appearance in 1986, however.

The Heritage Softail was an unashamed replica of Harley's 1949 FLH Hydra Glide, complete with pseudo-hardtail frame, deeply valanced mudguards, and optional fringed leather panniers. Sensibly, white plastic panniers were *not* on offer this time. Though priced at the top end of the range, the superbly detailed Heritage soon found a ready market. Fitted with performance add-ons from the company's recently introduced 'Screaming Eagle' selection of tuning parts, the Heritage could even be made to move with what many might consider to be indecent haste for such a gentlemanly conveyance.

Rather more curious was the company's 1988 decision to reintroduce springer forks on the FXSTS Springer Softail, a full eighty years after their first appearance on the front of a Harley-Davidson and, more significantly perhaps, forty years after they had made an unlamented departure in favor of telehydraulic forks. Although almost universally praised in its homeland, some non-American testers found the Springer's skinnily-tired front end to be a trifle unpredictable, not to say skittish, in damp conditions. Such criticisms as there were went largely unnoticed amid another enthusiastic take-up by the growing numbers of motorcyclists in search of something a bit different.

Niggles aside, the Springer is an appropriate machine on which to wrap up this condensed history of one of the world's most charismatic automotive marques, for it typifies the weird dichotomy behind Harley-Davidson's current success. The idea of putting new wine in distinguished-looking old bottles might sound less than honest, but if the wine is good enough to carry off the subterfuge, who are we to complain? And, like fine wines, Harley-Davidsons possess a unique capacity to improve with the passing of the years. Long may the vintages continue to be laid down.

Insignia and artefacts are an inseparable part of the Harley-Davidson experience, and identify the wearer as a believer in the true way. Again, the factory has legitimised this aspect of the sport by producing its own range of highly profitable geegaws. You can even buy removable tattoos now for that street-credible look in the bars at Daytona Beach.

Engraving, gold plating, even jewel-encrusting – there are no limits, either aesthetic or financial, to what some Harley owners will do to their trusty steeds. In the modern age of factory-prepared 'customs', it is becoming increasingly difficult to make your own personal statement, but that doesn't mean you can't try. . .

There is no doubting the talent of many customisers, particularly in the United States, where there exists a wide and sophisticated range of painting and plating facilities. One positive upshot of the factory's recognition of these customer desires has been a continual rise in the quality of their own painting, which is now second to none.

Every February, thousands of motorcycling enthusiasts from all over the world congregate in Daytona, Florida. Ostensibly, the event is a week long series of road races held inside the Daytona speedbowl, but in practice the vast majority of spectators are there for the social scene, to cruise downtown bars. . . or simply to watch one another.

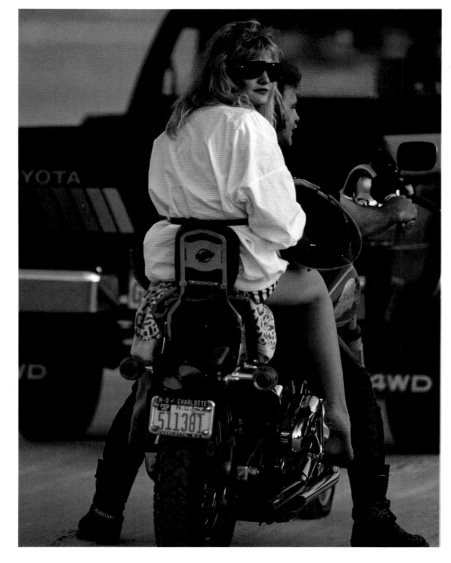

Selected Specifications

	JD/JDH 61 & 74 cu.in.	61-E	Hydra-Glide	XL Sportster	Duo-Glide	Electra-Glide	FX Super Glide
First Year of Manufacture	1928	1936	1949	1957	1958	1965	1971
Engine Type	Twin Cam	Knucklehead	Panhead	XL-Shovel	Panhead	Panhead (1965) Shovelhead (1966 on)	Shovelhead
Capacity	1000/1200cc	1000cc	1200cc	883cc	1200cc	1200cc	1200cc
Bore and Stroke (inches)	3.31×3.50/ 3.41×3.50	3.31×3.50	3.43×3.96	3.00×3.81	3.43×3.96	3.43×3.96	3.43×3.96
Horsepower Rating (claimed)	8.68hp/9.5hp	40bhp	55bhp	40bhp	55bhp	60bhp	65bhp
Transmission	3 speed	4 speed	4 speed	4 speed	4 speed	4 speed	4 speed
Weight (wet)	575lbs	600lbs	600lbs	500lbs	600lbs	780lbs	575lbs
Top Speed (est)	90mph	98mph	100mph	85mph	100mph	97mph	99mph

	XR 750 (Alloy)	FXS Low Rider	FLT Tour Glide	FXB Sturgis	FXRS Low Glide	FXST Softail
First Year of Manufacture	1972	1978	1980	1980	1982	1985
Engine Type	XL-Shovel	Shovelhead	Shovel/Evo	Shovelhead	Shovel/Evo	Evolution
Capacity	750cc	1200cc	1340cc	1340cc	1340cc	1340cc
Bore and Stroke (inches)	3.12×2.98	3.43×3.96	3.50×4.25	3.50×4.25	3.50×4.25	3.50×4.25
Horsepower Rating (claimed)	90bhp	65bhp	65bhp	65bhp	65bhp	65bhp
Transmission	4 speed	5 speed	5 speed	4/5 speed	5 speed	4 speed
Weight (wet)	320lbs	640lbs	795lbs	630lbs	640lbs	650lbs
Top Speed (est)	130mph	100mph	98mph	100mph	102mph	108mph

Left: The ultimate expression of luxury touring – the FLT Tour Glide.

Index

Picture Credits

The Bettmann Archive pages 22 below, 32 top, 50 top
EMAP Archives, Peterborough pages 8-9, 12-13, 14, 20-21 both, 22-23, 25 top, 26, 27 top, 40-41, 42-43, 49 below, 53 top, 59 both, 60-61 both, 64, 66-67, 68-69, 83
Bob Jones Jr. Inc. pages 1, 55 below, 70 top, 91 top, 101, 103 right, 104 top, 105 top, 106-107 all five, 108-109 all five
Grant Leonard pages 95, 110
Julian Mackie pages 75 top, 92 below, 97, 98
Julian Mackie/*Superbike* page 94 top
Andrew Morland pages 34-35, 39 below, 44-5 all three, 65 top, 73 top, 84, 86 top, 89 top, 100 right, 102, 103 left and below, 104 below, 105 below
Don Morley pages 2-3, 12, 15, 23, 24, 28-29, 31, 32 below, 38, 50 below, 58 both, 62-63, 65 below, 66, 68 top
National Motor Museum, Beaulieu pages 4-5, 10, 16-17, 18, 19, 25 below, 27 below, 30-31, 33, 36-37, 46-47, 48, 49 top, 52, 53 below, 80-81, 82-83, 85 below, 86 below
Springer/Bettmann Film Archive page 57
Bert Shepard/Silver Shutter pages 6, 41, 72-73, 76, 78, 79, 87 right, 90 below
Gary Stuart pages 7 both, 36, 51, 69, 70 below, 71, 72, 74, 75 below, 77, 85 top, 88, 89 below, 90 top, 91 below, 94 below, 96, 99 both, 100 left and below
Gary Stuart/Performance Bikes pages 92 top, 93
UPI/Bettmann Newsphotos pages 11, 30, 39 top, 87 left